A Girl's Guide to

Best Friends

AND mean Girls

DANNAH GRESH
& SUZY WEIBEL

HARVEST
Kids™

HARVEST HOUSE PUBLISHERS
EUGENE, OREGON

All Scripture quotations in part 1 are from the Holy Bible, New Living Translation, copyright © 1996, 2004, 2015 by Tyndale House Foundation. Used by permission of Tyndale House Publishers, Inc., Carol Stream, Illinois 60188. All rights reserved.

All Scripture quotations in part 2 are from the first edition of the Holy Bible, New Living Translation, copyright © 1996 by Tyndale House Foundation. Used by permission of Tyndale House Publishers, Inc., Carol Stream, Illinois 60188. All rights reserved.

Cover and interior design by Julia Ryan

Interior illustrations: Julia Ryan (except: pages 42 and 43 by Andy Mylin); some spot illustrations © Shutterstock.com

HARVEST KIDS is a trademark of The Hawkins Children's LLC. Harvest House Publishers, Inc., is the exclusive licensee of the trademark HARVEST KIDS.

TRUE GIRL is a registered trademark of Dannah Gresh.

A GIRL'S GUIDE TO BEST FRIENDS AND MEAN GIRLS
Copyright © 2008, 2013 by Dannah Gresh
Published by Harvest House Publishers
Eugene, Oregon 97408
www.harvesthousepublishers.com

ISBN 978-0-7369-8199-6 (pbk.)
ISBN 978-0-7369-8200-9 (eBook)

The Library of Congress has cataloged the edition as follows:
Library of Congress Cataloging-in-Publication Data
Gresh, Dannah.
A girl's guide to best friends and mean girls / by Dannah Gresh and Suzy Weibel.
          pages cm—(Secret Keeper Girl series)
ISBN 978-0-7369-5531-7 (pbk.)
ISBN 978-0-7369-5532-4 (eBook)
1. Friendship—Religious aspects—Christianity. 2. Girls—Religious life. I. Title.
BV4647.F7G725 2013
241'.676208342—dc23
                                                          2012048467

Printed in the United States of America

20 21 22 23 24 25 26 27 28 / VP / 10 9 8 7 6 5 4 3 2 1

To all our
True Girl fans.
We love meeting
you when we get
the chance!

This book on friendship took a lot of friends to write! And we want to say thanks to those friends and to God for giving them to us.

First, we are thrilled to thank God for the friendship he has given us in each other. It's so fun to get to work with one of your best friends!

It's also a lot of fun to work with people who are friends with Jesus, and that makes us good friends no matter how far apart we may live. The friends who have worked hard on this project include LaRae Weikert, Terry Glaspey, Barb Sherrill, and more. They are part of the team at our publisher, Harvest House. Our friends Julia Ryan and Andy Mylin made this book fantastic by designing it to be beautiful!

And thanks to our best friends on this earth, Bob and Jonathan, our husbands.

But mostly thanks to the best friend a girl can have, Jesus! We hope you meet him in the pages of this book or get to hang with him like you never have before.

Contents

A Note from Dannah and Suzy . . . 6

PART ONE:
About BFFs and Mean Girls

Chapter 1	Choosing Your Team	10
Chapter 2	Being a Friend	14
Chapter 3	Green with Envy	18
Chapter 4	The Wounds of a Friend	23
Chapter 5	Crazy but True: I Can Be Jesus' Friend!	29
Chapter 6	The Friend of a Friend	35

PART TWO:
My Best Friend, Jesus—Bible Study

	Getting Ready to Dig In to Bible Study	42
Meditation 1	How Did Jesus Pick Friends for Keeps?	51
Meditation 2	How Did Jesus "Do" Friendship?	61
Meditation 3	What Did Jesus Do When His Friends Got Jealous?	70
Meditation 4	What Did Jesus Do When His Friends Hurt Him?	81
Meditation 5	How Can I Be a Good Friend to Jesus?	88
Meditation 6	Who Needs to Meet My Friend Jesus?	96

Do You Know Jesus? . . . 109

Extra Ideas for Bible Study . . . 110

Answers to Puzzle Crazes! . . . 111

A Note from Dannah and Suzy

Friendships sure can be messy. We know. We're friends, and sometimes we're messy.

Maybe you have some friendships that are messy. Mean-girl moments? Jealousy? BFF tug-of-war? Well, that's why we wrote this book. We've experienced all those things and lived to tell about it.

{ **It's going to be okay.** }

God's Word gives us really clear guidelines about friendships and examples of people who knew how to handle friendship. But the hard part about reading the Bible is applying it to the life you live today. So, we've created the True Girl Series. These books are part modern-girl self-help and part Bible study, so you can think through how God's truth can work in your real life.

That's Suzy on the left side. She's a super cool, brown-haired tomboy who can shoot hoops with the best of the guys but also thinks it's great to be a girl and would not have it any other way.

And that's Dannah on the right. She's a natural born blonde who lives on a hobby farm with horses, llamas, fainting goats, peacocks, one lonely mini-donkey, and her beloved dog, Moose.

Suzy & Dannah

PART 1 of this book—about BFFs and Mean Girls— is "self-help" but we like to call it God-help.
(This part of the book was written by Suzy.)

Self-help is the kind of book your parents read when they want to be a better parent or bookkeeper or gardener. In this case, you're reading it because you want to know how to be a better friend. Self-help books advise you on certain topics. You'll read a lot of them in your lifetime.

To be honest, we don't love what bookstores call this "genre." (That's the big word they use to describe a certain kind of book.) Because we are not going to offer you help you can do yourself. We just don't think the answer is ever within ourselves. So, we like to call our books God-help books.

Don't worry if this is your first of its kind. You may be more used to chapter books and fiction. So Suzy's written it in that style and it will be fun to read. You can do this part of the book alone.

PART 2 of this book—My Best Friend, Jesus— is a Bible study.
(This part of the book was written by Dannah.)

A Bible study guides you through God's Word on a certain topic or book and enables you to do your own studying. You'll be reading Bible verses and answering questions about them, applying them to your life. There are even quizzes and games in the second section. It's going to be fun. You have to put some work in to feel the thrill in your belly for this kind of fun! You can do the second part of the book alone, but it's much better if you do it with your mom or a group of other girls.

PART 1

ABOUT
BFFs
AND **mean**
Girls

BY SUZY WEIBEL

Choosing Your Team

She breezed into my sixth-grade life about as smoothly as the Pacific winds that had taught her to surf. She had it all, from hair bleached by California sunshine to the perfect feathered bangs. She was pretty, she had a West-Coast wardrobe—and man, could she play ball!

I had grown up with two older brothers, and I was quite the tomboy. I had to do everything just like they did, from eating a ton of food to doing a flip off the top of the slide into the deep end of our pool. We walked on split-rail fences, jumped out of trees, and played a lot of football in the backyard. When I was 11, I was the first girl in my town to play Little League baseball. The funny thing is that through all of this I had a pink bedroom and loved to play with Barbie dolls. There is a line in a song we used to play during our True Girl pre-show that says, "We play football, we wear pink"! That describes the sixth-grade me to a T. I had a hard time finding other girls who were just like me—but then, like I said, Bobbi breezed into my life.

I knew other girls who liked sports and I had other girls to play Barbie with…but Bobbi somehow felt like an extension of me. We could complete sentences for each other. We liked to eat—a lot—shoot pool, take long walks, throw a football back and forth, and shop for clothes. And, did we ever like boys.

You can tell a lot about a person from the friends they choose. Friends not only reflect who we are, but they also say a lot about who we are becoming. I always considered Bobbi the leader in our relationship. She was more of an extrovert (she thrived on being around a lot of people), while I was a little quieter. She was the idea person and I was the one who made things happen.

Once Bobbi decided we should soap windows on Halloween. We gathered up our soap and snuck around in the night drawing soapy pictures on the windows of homes with no lights on. Every time we heard a car or voices, or were caught in the sudden flicker of a porch light, we would head giggling for the nearest ditch. (We probably would not do that again today.) Our escapades were sometimes foolish, but we were headed the same direction in life. We loved our families, we loved school, and we were honestly trying to love God too. We were just a little fuzzy in our decision making now and then! Today we are both pastors' wives. How about that!

Think
ABOUT IT

The most popular kids, the ones who kind of rule the school, are not often the ones who make the biggest splash in the world as adults. A lot of influential people, in fact, have reported being very unpopular in school.

My Friend Choice

Every choice in life impacts us, not just our friendships. For instance, when I go to a restaurant, I get to choose what I order, right? (Well, unless Mom and Dad are paying the bill. Then that big old steak may not be an option!) If I order something I'm allergic to, there will be a consequence. It will change the status of my health. If my eyes are bigger than my tummy, food goes to waste. It's never good to waste food.

Not every decision we make is life-altering. But it's good to be aware of the truth. Friends will change you, mold you, impact you, and either help or hinder you along the way.

Do you know what a "queen bee" is? Some call her a mean girl. She is the girl who rules over all the other "wanna-bees." She may be regarded as the prettiest or the coolest girl of all, but the way she has achieved her reputation is *not* pretty. She is the queen and she knows it. If anyone threatens her position at the top, she will quickly arrange for all of the other girls to help her send a strong message...you are *out* of the group. Now that's mean! When looking to choose your team of friends, the queen bee is not likely to be a good first pick.

Think ABOUT IT

A true friend is one who chooses friendship over popularity, money or image.

. . . .

I sometimes protected other girls from the queen bee when I was in school. I knew enough not to think she could be my true friend, though I tried to be friends with everyone. I do remember one day I gave the "queen bee" a piece of gum and was glad to do so. It's nice when the most popular girl in school talks to you...well, that's what I thought. Later in the day, thinking that stick of gum had sealed our friendship, I approached the "queen" and another popular girl. I was well-liked myself, so I was surprised when the two girls turned their backs on me and giggled. I guess they were mean girls too. It was intentional and it was mean. I went home and wrote in my diary, "See if I ever give her a stick of gum again. Who does she think she is?"

A lot of girls are confused by the queen bee. It seems she would be the best kind of friend to have, because she defines "popular." But "popular" isn't real. It can't be measured, it's more of an opinion, it is always changing, and it definitely isn't what Jesus was looking for in friends.

Jesus' Friend Choice

Jesus says this about you: "I no longer call you slaves, because a master doesn't confide in his slaves. Now you are my friends, since

I have told you everything the Father told me" (John 15:15). Does it amaze you that He says that about you? In the very next verse Jesus points out that we didn't choose him. He chose us. He picked you to be his friend. So here we have the King of kings and he has chosen *you* as a friend. I don't know about you, but I'm really nothing special. I'd think the King would want to have movie stars and great athletes, presidents and other kings for his best buddies...but he has chosen us.

choose your own team

You get to choose your own team when it comes to friends. No one else can do it for you. And Jesus gave us a great lesson in friend selection by choosing us. He didn't pick the most popular or powerful people to make him look better. No, Jesus chose his friends carefully.

There were a lot of people who wanted to be with him, but he knew that not all of them had what it took to be a good friend. One guy in Matthew 19 came to Jesus promising that the two of them had a lot in common. He had kept all of God's commandments and had great wealth. Like many people, he suspected Jesus was a king, and who doesn't want to be the king's buddy? But Jesus knew one thing about this potential friend—he would always put his money ahead of his friendship with Jesus.

It's tempting, isn't it, to choose friends based on how important they seem? Some girls spend hour after painful hour trying to prove they belong with the "in" crowd. If Jesus didn't waste his time there, maybe we shouldn't either! Instead, he looked for people who were simple, quiet, loyal, steady...and in need of friends. We all need friends. Jesus needed them too. I think it's an awesome thing that he taught us how to look for true friends!

Really
THINK ABOUT IT!

Go to Meditation #1 in Part 2: How did Jesus pick friends for keeps?

2

Being a Friend

Bobbi flat out knew I struggled with liking myself. She could see it. She heard me talking about it. And it made her sad, because she really and truly loved me. She made a habit of telling me how pretty I was, how much she liked being with me…nothing seemed to help. In eighth grade Bobbi even bought me a mirror that said, "I'm Gorgeous" all around the frame. I confessed to my diary the mirror wasn't doing me any good.

Both of us were so eager to make friends and be liked we sometimes made bad decisions. One night, Bobbi called to tell me that a girl known for being a bit of a "bad girl" at school had called her and wanted her to skip school with her the next day. Bobbi was hesitant. This kind of thing wasn't in our DNA—it didn't come naturally to either of us. But that's the thing about wanting friends sooooo badly—you tend to lose all sense of reason. Anything to be liked!

Fortunately, I was able to convince Bobbi what a dumb idea skipping school would be. I reminded her of all the trouble she could get into and how important it was to have the trust of our parents and teachers. All of that goes away if you skip school! Plus, did she want to get the same reputation the other girl had? What happened next was actually kind of funny. Bobbi snapped back to her senses so hard that she ran downstairs and fell into her parents' arms, confessing to them what she had almost done.

Even though Bobbi's family moved thousands of miles away after eighth grade, she and I went through a lot of highs and lows, celebrations and tears together. We kept each other's secrets and occasionally found ways to close the distance and spend time together. We still do.

One of the main things the Bible sets out to teach us is how to be a friend. Jesus calls us friends, and his word is a blueprint for how to be just like him. So there you have it—the Bible is one of the world's premiere textbooks on how to be a friend!

There are a lot of keys to good friendships. Friendships take work, just like everything else that's alive and breathing! You can't forget to water a plant, or soon you'll find a pot full of dried-up twigs you might just mistake for an earring tree! A new puppy has to be fed and walked and played with or you will have a disobedient monster on your hands. Here are a few areas where Jesus taught us to throw ourselves into friendships.

Euripides said, "It is a good thing to be rich, and it is a good thing to be strong, but it is a better thing to be loved of many friends." Euripides was a classical Greek author who lived almost 500 years before Jesus!

. . . .

Area 1: Time

Can you imagine trying to convince someone you like them if you never make time for them? Wouldn't really fly, would it?

Friendships thrive on time spent together. The very wise Winnie the Pooh said, "If you live to be a hundred, I want to live to be a hundred minus one day, so I never have to live without you." Researchers tell us that people who spend time with friends experience more happiness than people who are lonely! That's no real surprise, is it? And happiness is good for our health. Therefore...spending time with friends is good for us. Proverbs 17:22 actually says "a cheerful heart is good medicine"!

Area 2: Influence

"The heartfelt counsel of a friend is as sweet as perfume and incense" (Proverbs 27:9). Have you ever had a friend who was a bad influence on you? That's a pretty common experience, because  friends tend to influence our behavior more than anyone else once we reach a certain age. One thing unique about Jesus and his friendships is he did all the influencing. He had friends he hung out with, and homes he frequented for dinner and parties, but he was always talking to his friends about the kingdom of God.

You can be an influencer too. In fact, if you are a good friend you'll always be cheering on what is best for your buddies. Be sure your friends are able to encourage you using truth from God's Word. But if you have a friend (or two) who doesn't know God (having a friend like that isn't a bad idea, really) just be sure she is willing to *hear* God's Word. If a girl wants nothing to do with truth, she's not going to make great friend material just yet. There are some relationships that need to be put on a back burner or out to pasture...and we need to know there is nothing ungodly about that.

Area 3: "Co-Misery"

"Co" is a prefix meaning "together"...and we all know what misery is, don't we? You have cried. I have cried. Misery. Doing it together is to "commiserate." There's your big vocab word of the day!

When a friend is hurting we often feel uncomfortable. What do you say to make it all go away or feel better? The truth is, words aren't likely to do the trick. When a friend is hurting, the best thing we can do is stay by their side and simply hurt with them. You may think saying things like "It'll be okay" or "Things will get better" are most helpful, but the most helpful response is to do what Jesus did. He wept. When he lost his friend Lazarus, he and the others who loved Lazarus mourned together. They just cried.

Area 4: Prayer

Do you pray for your friend? Do you pray with her? Granted, praying out loud is not the most comfortable thing in the world for many people, but prayer is a sign of authentic friendship.

What to pray? Pray that she will love God with her whole heart. Pray she will be a good friend to you and you to her. Pray she will make good choices. Pray she will realize when God gives her good things, that she will work hard, and that she will know she is loved by God. Pray about everything!

Really THINK ABOUT IT!

Go to Meditation #2 in Part 2: How did Jesus "do" friendship?

Your friend-prayers don't have to be long or fancy. Just talk to God like you talk to your friends. This should be easy to do, seeing as he counts you as one of his friends. Why is prayer so important? Because without Jesus *we can't do anything*...including be a good friend! Maybe this is why we see so many friendships falling apart. What do you think?

When we love our friends in these four areas, we can know for certain we are the real deal. These are the things a friend does. This is how a friend loves. After all, there is only one true motivation for friendship, and that is *love*.

Green with Envy

Before you go and think Bobbi and I had the perfect friendship, let me set the record straight. I have never had a friendship in my life that has been perfect.

Growing up, I had always been the best girl athlete around.

Suddenly, along came Bobbi, and my reign as queen of the court was severely challenged! I became *jealous* of her. She was supposed to be my friend, not the competition. But I just couldn't help being jealous if she got more playing time than I did or when she scored more points than I did. I wanted her to do well and I was proud she was my friend, but at the same time I was hoping she would fall a little short so I could be the hero. How could such an ugly war be raging inside of me? I knew right then and there that I was facing my own battle about whether to be a mean girl. Or not.

I wasn't the only jealous one either. Bobbi and I lived in the same town for just two years. Her family was there so her dad could go to seminary. In her mind, her family was poor and mine was rich. She loved to come sleep in my huge bedroom, sit in the hot tub, and go on vacation with my family. Because she was the new kid, she experienced all of the typical problems new kids face when trying to make friends. She didn't like it when I had other girls spend the night or made plans to be at another girl's house for the weekend—she felt like she was losing her position in my life. She shouldn't have worried, but that's jealousy for you: born of insecurity. It's also what births mean girls.

Jesus' Friends Get Jealous

The good news is, Jesus gave us an example of how to deal with jealousy, and he has definitely provided a way out for you! He had 12 guys (the disciples) whom he had called to follow him. They had left everything to do what he'd asked, which is a great display of faith, but things weren't perfect in their little tribe. Remember, these were human friendships just like your own. Three of these guys were a little closer to Jesus than the others, namely Peter, James, and John. Being frail human beings ourselves, we completely understand that the other nine were a little jealous over this situation.

To make matters worse, two of Jesus' best buds wanted to be sure they would have those same positions of favor nailed down once Jesus started ruling as a king. They had their mom ask if they could sit on thrones beside him. You heard right—their mom did their dirty work. To be fair to the boys, they had just heard Jesus say the disciples would sit on 12 thrones with him in eternity, but they just didn't understand yet. They thought they were special because they traveled around with Jesus

Have you ever read a book where the main character (the protagonist—otherwise known as the good guy) is all twisted up by jealousy? Why is it always a minor character, and a troublemaker at that, who stirs up things by trying to make people jealous of each other? In real life, both the good guy and the bad guy suffer from bouts of jealousy.

. . . .

and he was kind of a rock star. People would flock from all over to see Jesus and hear him teach.

Fame sounded good to the disciples. What they didn't know… *yet*…was that those same crowds would turn on Jesus and take his life from him. They didn't know that one day they would give their *own* lives in the same way he had. They didn't know they would sit on those thrones not because they were best friends with a rock star, but because they had remained faithful to him even to their deaths.

✳

THINK
ABOUT IT

What might happen if I remind a friend who feels insecure how much she means to me instead of snapping at her?

. . . .

Of course the other disciples were offended by the request of James and John, but why do you think they were upset? Do you think it was because they loved James and John and hated to see them sinning? Or is it possible they were upset by…feelings of jealousy? You'd better believe it was jealousy! So Jesus had to do something quickly to put everyone in their proper places and right minds again, and this is where we can learn from him.

What Jesus Does to Help

Knowing jealousy is born out of insecurity, Jesus reminds the guys they are still part of his plan. He doesn't get snarky with them or tell them how stupid their question was. He says something like "Knock it off, you goofballs. Every last one of you is going to get your chance at greatness. And you are all my best buds, even though you have no idea yet what that means!"

One of the worst things you can do when you or a friend are having a jealousy meltdown is to ignore the situation. Be very careful, because this is exactly what other friends may encourage you to do. Dannah and I can remember so many times in school when one girl would play us against another. One friend wanted us

to spend the night but another had alre[ady]
had won the "battle of the sleepover" w[...]
whisper, "Come on. Let's go. She's just [...]
wound of being left out cut the jealous [...]

Jesus spent a lot of time alone with [...]
This gave the others plenty of opportu[...]
prevented a big civil war among his frie[...]
jealousy arose among Jesus' three amig[...]
gang together and reminded them of one important thing [...]
don't do things in the kingdom of God the way the rest of the
world does things.

Figuring Out Where You Belong

James and John were not kings. If we look back to their
humble beginnings, we find them in a boat repairing their nets
when Jesus first called to them. They owned a good business with
their dad. They had a few boats and a few hired men,
and they did a lot of trade in the city, which
meant James and John could probably speak
several languages. They were no dummies.
But they weren't kings, either. Not a speck of
royal blood flowed through these boys' veins.
Yet they wanted to rule with Jesus.

we want to be the star!

Isn't this just like jealousy? We want to be
like the star in the school play, but we forget she has taken dance
classes every day after school since she was five. We hate the fact
that one girl scores all the points for our basketball team, but while
we're home watching cartoons she's still at the gym practicing her
shooting. And doesn't it stink when someone gets to travel all over
the world and your family has never even left the state? Yet they did
not choose to be born into privilege any more than you chose to be
born in the United States instead of to peasants in some poverty-
stricken region of the world.

...nd you to look again at Jesus. He was the King ...y was everything in the world created for him, ...m. He happens to have the most important name in ...d. Angels worship him. Instead of keeping all that to ..., he chose to share it with you. James and John wanted to ...with him, and do you know where he pointed them? To their ...nees. We rule with Jesus when we wash people's feet. We are his princesses when we serve others and put them before ourselves.

Every fairy-tale movie shows us a girl living the life that every other girl envies. And who doesn't want to be the belle of the ball now and then? Sometimes it's fun to watch the royal family in England and wonder what it would be like to have crowds line up for days just to catch a glimpse of you. What if you had the finest designers making beautiful, one-of-a-kind dresses for you to wear and if every time you stepped onto the street thousands of lights flashed on cameras?

Just remember that Jesus, who deserved every award and title ever known to man, did not allow his friends to envy his position. He joined them instead in a new position. Humility is the invitation Jesus makes to you and me. We don't get to be waited on hand and foot, envied, or pampered. We get to serve.

Really
THINK ABOUT IT!

Go to Meditation #3 in Part 2: What did Jesus do when his friends got jealous?

A Girl's Guide to Best Friends and Mean Girls

The Wounds of a Friend

She wouldn't quit following me! I'm an introvert to begin with, meaning I need a lot of time and space to myself. But on top of everything else she was weird. She cramped my style. She didn't really hang out with the group...she hovered around us. She laughed a little too loudly and usually when no one else was laughing. It was obvious she was trying too hard to fit in.

I tried moving over to the girls near the swing set. She skipped along beside me. I excused myself to visit the girls playing foursquare. Did she think we were attached at the hip or something? I couldn't shake her! Finally, I snapped. "Leave me alone! Why do you have to follow me everywhere? Don't you have other friends you can latch on to?"

The moment the words were out of my mouth I regretted them. I knew the answer. She didn't have other friends. The reason she was following me was for this very reason: I was the only one who had offered friendship. I was the only one who invited her to sit at lunch, to play a board game during indoor recess, or who made room for her on the bus seat. I was her friend, and now I had delivered the first punch.

God Made Us to Have Friends

When God created the earth and all that is in it, he made it very clear he is a God who loves community. What this means is that he values relationships as much as you and I do. He has always been a "triune" God—Father, Son, and Holy Spirit. Even though he has existed from before the beginning of time, he has never been alone. He is three persons, one God. When Adam and Eve were created from the dust and took their first breath, their eyes were opened to a God who wanted to be with them.

Think ABOUT IT

Kids were not the ones who invented the concept of "hanging out"... God was.

. . . .

We thrive on being with other people from the time we are babies. As a matter of fact, a scientist at Harvard (yep, the fancy-schmancy Ivy League school) conducted a study on baby monkeys. He wanted to see what would happen if they were not allowed to have any contact with others at birth.

He put together three groups of baby monkeys. The first he allowed to be with their mommies from the get-go. These babies had no problems learning how to be monkeys—they were good at nursing, cuddling, playing, and being corrected by their moms. As they grew older, they got along well with others and became loving parents themselves.

The next group of monkeys was "raised" by a wire replica of a monkey that was covered with soft fur and rigged with a bottle that provided milk. Though the "mother" monkey wasn't real (and therefore couldn't put her arms around the baby or correct her behavior) the babies were able to snuggle for warmth and felt safe hiding behind the fur-covered mommy when frightened. These monkeys were not quite as good at meeting new friends. They tended to get into more fights and were slower to trust, but they eventually adjusted, and most grew up to be good parents.

The final group was the one who got the bad deal. These monkeys were "raised" by a wire monkey rigged with a bottle of milk...but no fur. This "mom" was not able to cuddle, correct, or even provide warmth and comfort for the babies. They were afraid of this wire monster and would approach only to get milk. They spent the rest of their time in the opposite corner of the cage. When introduced to new monkeys, these babies could not play or interact. They often picked fights. As they grew up, they were unable to be parents themselves.

It's a sad story, but what the researchers found out was very valuable in helping scientists, psychologists, parents, and pastors (and now you!) understand how unbelievably important interaction with others is. It's especially important that we have others to be *close* to. Cuddles are good! Even conflict is good, if we have it with people who love us.

When You Hurt a Friend

Growing up, both of us heard, "A true friend won't ever hurt you." But after a number of years we have decided this is not a completely true statement. If it's true, then we actually never loved the girls whom we hurt by being jealous. But we did love them! If it's true, then Peter didn't really love Jesus when he denied knowing him three times...but wouldn't you agree with us that Peter loved Jesus very much?

but we did love them!

Peter was a lot like you and me. (We know, we know. He was a guy, and probably even older than your dad. But that doesn't matter in this case.) He was a lot like you and me in his tendency to defend himself when he was afraid. He had just seen Jesus arrested and violently beaten. He knew Jesus was headed toward death at the hands of the Romans, and he didn't really understand the whole concept of resurrection just yet.

All he knew was if he identified with Jesus, he might get the same treatment. Peter panicked.

Think about the last time you hurt a friend. Maybe you ignored her out of fear that another group of girls would ditch you. Maybe you were afraid that being her friend would make you less popular. Maybe you decided nothing was worth being bullied or laughed at...not even her feelings.

Those fears were exactly what led me to hurt my friend on the playground that day. Do they sound familiar? Hopefully when we talk about Peter's fear and then the kind of fear we are willing to hurt friends over...our wounds will seem really small in comparison! Peter had a lot to fear. Then again, after Peter's denial, Jesus had a lot to forgive.

Do you know the rest of Peter's and Jesus' story? Of course, you know that Jesus did indeed die on a Roman cross, with only his mother, Mary, John, and a few others very nearby. The rest of his disciples watched from a distance. He was buried, and after three days God raised him from the grave. Peter and John heard a report of this and ran like madmen to the gravesite. The Bible says John ran faster than Peter—we have to wonder if this was all about athletic ability or if Peter was a little afraid to be face-to-face with Jesus after such a big mistake.

What Jesus Did with Peter

When Peter and Jesus finally did meet up again, what do you suppose Jesus did? He had a lot of options, that's for sure! He could have disowned Peter and informed him they weren't friends anymore. He could have turned the other disciples against Peter or pretended like he didn't know him. We're talking Jesus here, so he could even have called lightning down from heaven to snuff Peter out!

Jesus did none of these things. Those are the types of things you and I might do if we took advice from other people or went with our instincts. Those are what we might call reactions of our "flesh." In other words, these are the kinds of weak responses we might have had before we knew Jesus and before we put on his robes of righteousness. But now Jesus rules our lives, so it just makes sense to act like Jesus did.

Here's what Jesus did:

1 He helped Peter's fishing efforts. Peter was off fishing, probably trying to forget his sadness and grief. His best friend had died, and the last thing he had done was pretty much totally betray that friend. That's a very bad week. But Jesus told Peter where to place his nets in order to catch a ton of fish. He didn't lecture him or scold him. He helped him.

✳

THInK
ABOUT IT

Have you ever seen revenge restore a broken relationship?

2 He met Peter's needs for physical comfort. The Sea of Galilee is not exactly a tropical beach. I've been there. And it's not really a sea—it's a small freshwater lake! But the wind can blow cold and hard on this little lake, placing fishermen in great danger—and also causing them to freeze their behinds off! Peter, dampened by the spray and the water and hungry from a night of fishing, found a roaring fire and a fresh breakfast prepared by Jesus.

3 Finally, Jesus told Peter he still loved him. He told him three times...one for each time he had denied Jesus.

There's something else Jesus did here that is difficult to catch as a speaker of English, but you'd see it clearly enough if you spoke Greek. Here's how Jesus might have said it if he had spoken

English. He asks Peter two times, "Do you *truly* love me?" After both of these questions, Peter says, "Lord, you know I love you…" leaving off the word "truly." The third time Jesus simply says, "Peter, do you love me?"

Why did Jesus do this? We think it's because Peter had been bragging his head off earlier that he would follow Jesus anywhere. He pretty much thought he was the most faithful friend in the world. It would have been embarrassing for him to say, "I *truly* love you," after he had denied Jesus three times. Jesus brings Peter back to earth by getting him to admit that he loves like a human being. Weakly and with fault. Only Jesus is able to love *truly*, like God. Yep. Our human friends are going to disappoint us now and then.

Really Think ABOUT IT!

Go to Meditation #4 in Part 2: What did Jesus do when his friends hurt him?

Being like Jesus means more than forgiving. It means bringing our friends close to us again by loving on them. It's hard to love on someone who has hurt us. And no one knows that better than your best friend Jesus.

Crazy but True: I Can Be Jesus' Friend!

One time when I was in college I met a famous actor from a television show called *The Love Boat*. We bumped into one another in front of a Beverly Hills hotel, and the guy (who I knew just as Isaac—you can ask Mom or Dad about him) actually thought he knew me! He approached with a friendly smile and…I panicked! He was supposed to be on my TV screen, not two feet away from me! Suddenly the Suzy who is able to think quickly on her feet and talk for hours on end about anything was speechless.

When the actor said, "Hello," I responded with, "Hi, I…I…I'm nice."

When he asked how he knew me I stammered, "I'm no…no…nobody."

He climbed into his cab laughing, and I felt like crawling into a hole. There went one very cool adventure down the drain! But that's what fame does to us, more so than to the famous person. Most famous people would love to be treated like normal human beings. They would like to make friends based on things they have in common with others, but instead they have to deal with people who are so starstruck they can't even get around to "Hello, my name is Suzy."

Famous Friends

Have you ever wondered what it would be like to have a super-duper-famous friend?

All I know is it could be fun...A super-famous friend would probably be able to offer you unbelievable, once-in-a-lifetime experiences like big parties full of famous people or attending awards shows and being at the center of all those flashing paparazzi camera lights. She might have a really cool house on a cliff overlooking a beach or even a private airplane. She could afford to take you on vacations and shopping in stores you can't even afford to walk past! And face it, it's just fun to be able to say you know someone famous. It's one thing to meet someone famous...and it's a whole other thing to have their number in your cell phone. Pretty cool.

It could be awkward, though. Fame is kind of like quicksand. It looks solid, but once you step in it you find yourself being sucked under and scared. Your friend could be chased by photographers and magazines that say all kinds of mean and untrue things about her. She might have crazed fans writing scary things to her. It would be hard to be together with her in public because people would always be pointing, staring, whispering, and asking for autographs. Worst of all, she might have a hard time trusting friends. Do you like her for herself, or are you just a "friend" so you can take advantage of her fame? Famous people have a hard time maintaining good relationships, in case you haven't noticed.

The reality of a friendship with Jesus is just a little bit crazy. First of all, Jesus is a king, and not just any king at that. He is the King of kings. There is no name on earth greater than his. The Bible says that one day every single knee on earth will bow down to him and every voice will agree

Think
ABOUT IT

The most famous person ever to walk the face of this earth loves me and wants to be my friend.

. . . .

A Girl's Guide to Best Friends and Mean Girls

that he is the Ruler of everything. This is the One who wants to be friends with you. We guarantee there is no other friend you could have who would be more famous than Jesus. Talk about your "household name"! People may not understand who Jesus is—but it would be hard to find even one person who does not know that name.

We know how to be friends to the girls we go to school with. It's not too hard to befriend a neighbor. Even boys make a little bit of sense now and then. But how in the world are we supposed to be friends with the King of kings?

Fame is weird. All fame really means is "renown," or being known by everyone. The reason it is weird has less to do with the famous person and more to do with you and me. We don't know how to act when we get around famous people (like when I bumped into Isaac)!

THINK ABOUT IT

Do we have the faintest idea of how to be a friend... to Jesus?

....

Famous people have to travel in cars with tinted windows because we point and stare. They can't shop or eat in normal places because we interrupt them for autographs. It's simply not a normal life. We have a friend who has managed a lot of famous musicians' careers. He told us, "The weirdest day you will ever have in your life is what *every* day is like for the famous."

The Crazy-but-True Part

Jesus made it clear he thinks of us in terms of family and friendship. One time when his mom and his brothers were looking for him he asked,

 "'Who is my mother? Who are my brothers?' Then he pointed to his disciples and said, 'Look, these are my mother and brothers. Anyone who does the will of my Father in heaven is my brother and sister and mother!'" (Matthew 12:48-50).

Jesus didn't disown his mother and brothers. But he did include you and me in his family in a completely real way by making this statement. We define family by blood relations or adoption. Jesus does too, and he wants us to remember all who trust in him have been adopted into the family of God. You and I really are Jesus' sisters.

He also calls us friends now that we are part of his family:

66 "I no longer call you slaves, because a master doesn't confide in his slaves. Now you are my friends, since I have told you everything the Father told me" (John 15:15).

Being a Friend to Jesus

We've noticed that a lot of people have written about how Jesus is a good friend to us. Not many have tackled the question of how we can be a good friend to Jesus, but we figure if we look at how Jesus loves us, he can teach us how he wants to be loved.

1 Jesus wants to be with us. He was not a loner. He surrounded himself with 12 good buddies, but at one point he sent out 72 of his friends to tell people the good news that he was the Messiah. He was invited to weddings and to stay in people's homes. Friends spend time together, right? One way to be a good friend to Jesus, then, is to spend time with him. Talk to him! Spend time enjoying his presence as you look at what he has created. Look at all of the things he said (now recorded in the Bible) and make them personal. If you have a red-letter Bible, substitute your name in all of the verses printed in red. Write him letters. Be still and listen for his voice.

2 Jesus cares about us. He was funny, compassionate, patient, and emotionally attached to his friends. He flat-out wept when his friend Lazarus died. He called people by nicknames. What mattered to his friends mattered to Jesus.

3 We can trust Jesus. Titus 1:2 says it's impossible for God to lie. When he says something, we can count on it 100 percent. Jesus said when we prove to be trustworthy, he can use us for greater things. It's not that he needs us to do God's work. He doesn't. But it makes him really happy when we work alongside him. When we are trustworthy, working with Jesus is one of the big perks!

4 Jesus accepts us as we are. He had a lot of friends that other people thought he shouldn't have! He hung out with tax collectors— they were known to cheat people out of money. Some women with bad reputations hung around Jesus—he didn't chase them away. He was not being influenced by his friends' bad behavior—he was doing his Father's work by being with these people. We aren't exactly angels, you and I, but Jesus loves us anyhow.

THINK ABOUT IT

Do the things that matter to Jesus matter to me? Honesty? Righteousness? Truth? Honoring God? Obeying?

he accepts us as we are!

We can be his friends by accepting him as he is too. He is holy and perfect, he is the only way to heaven, he is the son of God…in fact, he is God. A lot of people try to change their friends and it just doesn't work. A lot of people also try to change who God is by saying things about him that just aren't true. The only way to really know Jesus inside and out is to read the Bible inside and out. Then when we talk to others about him, our best friend, we'll be able to describe him to a T!

5 Jesus set an example for us. This is the big one, so take some mental notes. Jesus made this simple. "If you love me, obey my commandments" (John 14:15). The book of Hebrews in the Bible says something really odd about Jesus. It says he learned obedience from the things he suffered (Hebrews 5:8). Jesus never sinned, right?

Why did he have to learn obedience? Here's the thing—he had to show us it could be done. And he had to show us what loving God looks like—it looks like obedience. Every time Jesus met a tough challenge, he was 100 percent obedient. Jesus loved his Father, and he obeyed. If we love him, we will do the exact same thing.

No one ever said it would be easy to be best friends with the King of kings! He's no ordinary guy. It's true his standards are a bit (okay, a ton!) higher than those of your other friends, but it's okay to have high standards when the rewards for friendship are also huge.

The Great Thing About Having Jesus as a Friend

Jesus says when we love him (obey) we produce "fruit." This isn't the produce-aisle, make-a-salad kind of fruit, but the kind of character traits that make us more and more like him. He said we know what people are like by the fruit their lives produce. A bad tree, he said, produces bad fruit. In fact, he said, a bad tree can't produce good fruit (Matthew 7:18-20)! That means a good tree can't produce bad fruit. One of the most awesome rewards of being Jesus' best friend is that he makes our fruit production pure goodness! Love, joy, peace, patience, kindness, gentleness, faithfulness, goodness, self-control...these are the words that begin to define us when we make it a habit to obey.

Does Jesus love us even when we don't obey? Yes, he does. He wants everyone to turn from disobedience and follow him. Disobedience prevents that good fruit from growing.

Really
THINK ABOUT IT!

Go to Meditation #5 in Part 2: How can I be a good friend to Jesus?

The Friend of a Friend

Is there any doubt peanut butter was made to go with jelly? Spaghetti isn't the same without meatballs. Dogs and cats go together. Biscuits and gravy go together. In fact, I have a dog named Biscuit and a cat named Gray-Vee. Designers make books better, coaches make athletes better, and recess makes the school day better!

Friends, by the way, were intended to make us better people. My friendship with Bobbi pushed me to be a better friend. I knew she was more faithful than I was, and that pushed me to want to be faithful too. I wanted her to meet the girls on my high-school baseball team (that's not a mistake—I played baseball rather than softball) when she came to visit me because she was a good athlete like they were. I knew they would have a lot in common and I figured meeting her would make their day brighter.

Friends Help Friends Help Friends . . .

I'm always trying to get my friends to meet my other friends. When I was younger, I sometimes let jealousy prevent this. But I hope you'll think carefully about this thing we now call "networking." The Bible says two people are always better than one because two people can help each other. Your friends can help each other with school, with meeting other kids who love Jesus, with finding ways to earn money in the summer—they can help each other get through tough times. Get in the habit now of introducing new friends to old ones. Incidentally, it is a characteristic of a mean girl to keep her friends to herself. That's not what God wants for you. Don't give in to the pressure to be jealous and controlling.

While it's almost always good to meet the friend of a friend, the Bible does speak of friendships in two ways. It speaks about bad friendships:

> "And if there is no resurrection, 'Let's feast and drink, for tomorrow we die!' Don't be fooled by those who say such things, for 'bad company corrupts good character.' Think carefully about what is right, and stop sinning. For to your shame I say that some of you don't know God at all" (1 Corinthians 15:32-34).

Do you choose your own friends? You'd better believe it! Oh, Mom and Dad have some input now, and it's right that they do. You need that kind of wisdom. What they are really doing is training you for the future when you will be 100 percent on your own in making new friends. They aren't trying to butt in—they are showing you the most excellent way to do friendship.

What to Do with Friendship Mistakes

We always say that bestselling books are written after big mistakes are made, and it's kind of true. The whole reason Dannah wrote her first book is because of a mistake she made in high school that God chose to redeem big time. But Dannah still had to go through the pain of that mistake. Fiction books aren't very good if there isn't a villain, and we don't have much in common with the heroine of the story if she doesn't first fall on her face. What we are trying to say is, if you make a friendship mistake it's not the end of the world. God can turn our disasters into runaway victories.

It's likely your parents have made friendship mistakes and have had to pay the price. You may not think it's such a big deal—after all, your mom and dad turned out fine in the end.

What if as a young child you had been warned not to play with the burners on the stove? It's hard to obey this rule because few things are as cool as an electric burner turned on high heat. Have you seen how the burner glows bright red? So one day Mom is fetching laundry from the basement and you decide to light up the burner. You are on a stepstool, passing your hand over the glowing stovetop, and you lose your balance. You put out your hands to catch yourself without even thinking...what happens?

THINK ABOUT IT

You can play with fire and live...but you may come out badly burned.

....

Well, when you are an adult you will warn your child about the stove. "Don't play with the stove—you may get burned," you will say. And she will look at your scars, the ones she has traced with her fingers for years, and think, *But you turned out okay.* Really? Even after seeing your scars she will think that? Yes. Because she never felt the pain. She didn't have to deal with hospitals and skin grafts...you get the idea. Your mom and dad have scars from bad choices in their past and *they do not want you to hurt like they did*!

 The Bible also celebrates good friend choices: "As iron sharpens iron, so a friend sharpens a friend" (Proverbs 27:17).

Making Good Friend Choices

Friends are supposed to make us better people. There are two famous authors you likely know of who did just that for one another. The setting was an English college town called Oxford, and the two young professors both taught English. After some time, J.R.R. Tolkien (author of *The Hobbit*) had shared enough of his faith that C.S. Lewis (author of the Chronicles of Narnia) placed his trust in Jesus too. Tolkien saw his writing as a pure hobby. He did it just for fun. But C.S. Lewis knew his friend was weaving great biblical truths into his stories, and he encouraged him to get them published. If it weren't for C.S. Lewis, the world might have never known the wonderful world of *The Hobbit*! But if it weren't for J.R.R. Tolkien, C.S. Lewis might have never known Jesus, his Savior.

We should be purposeful about our friend choices. Some people simply are not good for us.

- ♥ If I have to act like someone else to be around her, she is not a safe choice.

- ♥ If she wants me to gossip about others, she is not a good choice.

- ♥ If she pulls me away from things I love to do and people I love to be with, she is not the right friend.

- ♥ If I am growing more bad fruit than good because of her, she is not a good choice.

The Friend Choices Jesus Makes

Every once in a while, we don't choose friends—they choose us. Have you ever been minding your own business only to suddenly find the new kid at the lunch table beside you or shyly saying hello as she claims the desk next to you in class? Here's a funny side note about having Jesus as a best friend. In every single case, yours and ours included, Jesus is the one who chooses to be friends.

Think ABOUT IT

Did I pick all of my friends or did some of them pick me?

. . . .

The Bible says we did not choose him, but he chose us. He loved us first. His faithfulness is not a response to yours. If you worship harder or behave better, it doesn't make him love you more. He loved you before you ever heard his name... and he had already chosen you to be his friend. Because he's "omniscient" (that means he knows everything) he also knew you would befriend him in return.

This friendship of Jesus is fully amazing! He knew you back when he created the earth:

> "You watched me as I was being formed in utter seclusion, as I was woven together in the dark of the womb. You saw me before I was born. Every day of my life was recorded in your book. Every moment was laid out before a single day had passed" (Psalm 139:15-16).

He prayed for you when he was on the earth. Seriously! When he was offering up his last prayers just before his arrest and crucifixion, he prayed for you and me. This prayer was so personal it almost feels like he prayed for us by name:

> "I am praying not only for these disciples but also for all who will ever believe in me through their message. I pray that they will all be one, just as you and I are one—as you are in me, Father, and I am in you. And may they be in us so that the world will believe you sent me" (John 17:20-21).

ThInK ABOUT IT

How many of your friends do you think are thinking about you at this very second? What do you suppose they are thinking about?

· · · · · · · · · · · · · · · ·

According to the Bible's book of Hebrews, Jesus is sitting at God's right hand this very moment, still praying for you and for me. Jesus is serious about this friendship thing with us!

Jesus never stops thinking about you or talking to God about you on your behalf. The Bible says he "intercedes" for us. That's a big word, but in this case it means to meet with someone important and talk to them. And most of the time it is used when people have been summoned by a king for a conversation. Oh yeah! Jesus, the King of kings, is meeting with the Father and talking about *us*!

Good Friends Change Us in Good Ways

And now we have come full circle, back to where this chapter started. Friendship with Jesus is such a good thing we simply cannot keep it to ourselves. First of all, we shouldn't want to keep it to ourselves. When we like things, we talk about them.

Dannah likes her horses—she has photos of them everywhere and she loves to talk about them.

I love the Little League World Series—I talk about it nonstop every August.

We both have major crushes on our husbands, so you just might catch us gabbing about those cuties on a daily basis.

If we like something—if we are "into" it—we don't keep it a secret.

We also need to share our friendship with Jesus because he has "commissioned" us to do so. This means we have been given an order and the authority to make disciples, or followers of Jesus. He said,

> "Go and make disciples of all the nations, baptizing them in the name of the Father and the Son and the Holy Spirit. Teach these new disciples to obey all the commands I have given you. And be sure of this: I am with you always, even to the end of the age" (Matthew 28:19-20).

When friends ask us to do something for them, we do it, right? I can't begin to tell you all of the amazing adventures I've had out of loyalty to friends. I tried squid because a friend wanted me to. I waited an extra hour to ride in the front seat of the Millennium Force roller coaster at Cedar Point. I've gone to Germany twice for a friend. I have painted my nails a weird color, and I've gone parasailing.

Really Think ABOUT IT!

Go to Meditation #6 in Part 2: Who needs to meet my friend Jesus?

Why do we do things for friends? We do it because we really like them. We do it because we feel a loyalty to them. And we do it because we trust them. We'll never have another friend as awesome and true as Jesus, but in this way he is like our other BFFs—when he asks us to do something as a friend, we should be all in!

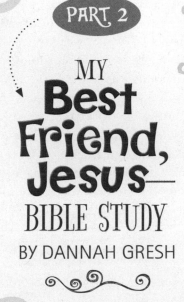

PART 2

MY
**Best
Friend,
Jesus**—
BIBLE STUDY

BY DANNAH GRESH

Getting Ready to Dig In to Bible Study

The front half of this book is full of stories and wisdom. But that's not enough. You have to dig for the rest of this treasure yourself. The Bible is God's love letter to...*you*! So roll up your sleeves and get ready to build on that foundation of yours. Jesus said it himself in Matthew 7:24-25—if we put his words into practice (if we are *doers*) we are building a house so strong that even the storms of life cannot take us down.

This True Girl series uses the powerful skill of *meditation* to help you dig in to God's Word. So before you start learning what the Bible says about best friends and mean girls, we'd like to take a little time to introduce you to meditation. (If you've done another book in the series, you can skip this if you want. But it will be great review—it offers new verses to help you practice meditation, and it will get you kick-started on this biblical study about best friends and mean girls.)

What Is Meditation?

You might think meditation is a crazy, weird thing you do while sitting cross-legged in a yoga position and humming. That's not true at all. That kind of meditation is just a sad fake for God's original. Let's see if we can help you get an idea of what God thinks meditation should look like.

Some Christians are so rigid about praying all the time that they never take time to study! Other Christians are so consumed with

STUDIER

Some Christians are really rigid about studying, studying, studying the Bible!

PRAY-ER

Some Christians are so consumed with praying all the time, they never study!

studying, studying, studying the Bible that they don't take time to pray! The risk for the **studier** is that her faith gets stuck in her head. She never has the *heart* to follow God because she is always arguing about or defending what she *thinks* about God.

The risk for the **pray-er** is that her faith is all about her heart. She makes decisions to follow God based on how she feels and forgets to think about what God has already told her in his written Word. (God will never ask you to do something that disagrees with the Bible.)

But then there's a third type of person. A meditator studies the Bible and then asks God to help her understand it while she prays. A

MEDITATOR

wise pastor once told me (Dannah) that meditation is what happens when studying and praying crash into each other!

I want to teach you to meditate. You need these things:

1. Your Bible. (You won't actually use it a lot, but that's because I'm keeping this study simple. All the verses you'll need are printed right in this book. But I want you to get into the habit of having your very own treasured Bible on hand!)

2. This copy of *A Girl's Guide to Best Friends and Mean Girls*.

3. Some colored markers or pencils.

........► These are your meditation tools. Got 'em? Okay.
      Let's just get them warmed up by practicing meditation.

Dig in
TO STUDY

DIG IN by Studying Psalm 119

Throughout this book, you'll see this symbol inviting you to "dig in." This means you are about to *study* God's Word, kind of like an archeologist studies the ground to uncover mysteries, secrets, and stories. So, plop on your hard hat and get ready to dig. Let's give it a try, okay?

First, let's do a little digging to see if God really does want us to practice meditation. After all, you shouldn't take my word for it. Psalm 119 is the loooooongest chapter in the Bible, and it's all *about* the Bible. I wonder if it talks about meditation. Let's find out. Read the Bible verses below with your pink marker in hand. Circle the word "meditate" in pink every time it shows up.

·········► Psalm 119

"Even princes sit and speak against me, but I will

meditate on your principles" (verse 23).

"Help me understand the meaning of your commandments,

and I will meditate on your wonderful miracles" (verse 27).

"I honor and love your commands.

I meditate on your principles" (verse 48).

"I will meditate on your age-old laws;

O LORD, they comfort me" (verse 52).

"Sustain me, and I will be saved; then I will

meditate on your principles continually" (verse 117).

So, does God want us to meditate? The answer is yes. The longest chapter in the Bible mentions it at least five times. Cool! But, just *what* does he want us to meditate on? Grab your purple marker. Circle in purple any words on the previous page that answer that question.

Now, fill in the blanks below by writing what we are supposed to meditate on, based on what you circled in purple.

1. _____ 3. _____

2. _____ 4. _____

We are supposed to meditate on God's principles (or basic rules), commandments, miracles, and age-old laws. Where can you find those things? In the Bible. Meditation always begins with studying the Bible, God's written Word to us.

How does it end? Let's take a peek. This is kind of like turning to the back page of your favorite True Girl fiction book to see how it ends. I don't recommend that if you're reading one of those, but in this case it'll give you determination to put the hard work into this Bible study.

Read the following verse and use your blue marker to circle the end result of meditation.

"Study this Book of the Law continually. Meditate on it

all day and night so you can be sure to obey all that is written in it.

Only then will you succeed" (Joshua 1:8).

What happens when we meditate on God's Word? We succeed. In fact, God makes a pretty bold promise to us. *Only then* will we succeed. Meditating on God's Word is your only way to claim God's promise to succeed.

Using all the markers you have, in the boxes below you can show three different areas where you'd really like to be successful. Maybe it's in your math class or on the soccer field. Maybe you'd like to be a successful pianist or a great friend. Draw a picture in each box.

puzzle craze

The Benefits of Meditation

Being *successful* is only one of God's promised outcomes for meditation. Let's look really hard at each verse we've been digging into. Using Joshua 1:8 and the verses from Psalm 119, find six words that describe the benefits of meditation. You'll use these to solve the crossword below.

For puzzle answers go to page 111.

········► CLUES

Each word describes you. (Big hint: Like the word *successful*!)

DOWN
1. Joshua 1:8
2. Psalm 119:52
4. Psalm 119:117

ACROSS
2. Psalm 119:23
3. Psalm 119:48
5. Psalm 119:27

LOOK inside yourself

After you "Dig In" by becoming a *studier* of the Bible, it's time to get ready to become a *pray-er*. I like to start by looking inside my own heart before I talk to God. This is kind of the bridge between studying and praying. When you see the "Look Inside" symbol, it means I'm getting ready to ask you some super-personal questions. Ready?

1 Put a check mark next to each quality that is true of you. I am or feel...

_____ SUCCESSFUL (with the things I do)

_____ CONFIDENT (enough to try new things and meet new people)

_____ OBEDIENT (to my parents, teachers, and God)

_____ STRONG (enough to keep going when I feel afraid)

_____ UNDERSTANDING (of God and others)

_____ COMFORTED (by God and my parents when things go wrong)

2 Fill in the blank by selecting one of the areas above where you hope God can change you.

I wish I were more _____ .

3 Now, here's the big one. How much time are you currently investing to meditate on God's Word each day? Remember, meditation includes studying the Bible *and* praying about what you have read! Circle one.

A. None

B. I spend some time reading or studying the Bible every day, but I don't pray very much. I need to pray more.

C. I pray every day, but I don't study the Bible very much. I need to start reading and studying regularly.

D. I spend a good amount of time both studying the Bible and praying. So, I am meditating. I'm not perfect, but I think I'm on track!

4 What do you think you need to do, based on what you've just studied while "digging in"?

Reach UP TO Talk TO GOD

When you see this graphic, you're going to add praying to your studying. Remember, you have not meditated until you've done both! I like to write my prayers down in a journal or diary. To help you learn how to do that, I'm going to help you write your prayers to God based on what we've just studied. First, fill in the blanks to personalize your prayer and then pray your prayer out loud.

Dear_____ (favorite name for

God), You are so _____ (your favorite

descriptive word for God)! I praise you for who you are! I

need to ask you to forgive me because I realize that I'm not

spending enough time _____

(studying your Word or praying) and I want to do better.

I know that there are a lot of benefits to meditating every day. Today when I studied those benefits, I realized that I wish I were more _____.

I am really struggling in this area and this makes me feel

_____.

Will you help me? As I start this True Girl Bible study, I promise to meditate by studying the Bible and then praying. I look forward to what you'll do in me to change me. I'm feeling very: _____ excited _____ overwhelmed.

I give this emotion to you.

In Jesus' name,

_____

(sign here)

Congratulations! You just meditated.

Now that you've practiced, we're ready to meditate on friendship and the greatest Friend ever!

MEDITATION 1

How Did Jesus Pick Friends for Keeps?

Oh, you just *hate* it when this happens! Your gym teacher has asked Trisha-the-All-Star and Julianne-the-Sure-to-Be-Soccer-Hero to pick teams for an all-girls game of kickball. Code pink alert! This is not going to go well. You've been here before. Sure enough, Trisha starts by picking her BFF, who's great at every sport. Julianne picks her total frenemy, a teammate who is sure to score. The slow, painful process of being the last one picked begins.

Relax! This is only a code pink *drill*. It's not the real thing! But does it sound familiar?

If it does, rest easy. You're not alone, and this Bible study is going to help you sort out stuff like that. There's an easy, scientifically valid test to take to find out if you are going to have friendship problems in your life. I'd like you to take it now.

Code Pink Quiz:

Are you a girl? CIRCLE ONE: . . . . . YES . . . . . NO

So, it's not really scientifically valid. I was just joking about that. But it is fairly accurate. Let's check your results!

If you circled "yes" (and I hope you did since you're a True *Girl*), you are going to face challenges in friendship. Mean-girl moments, getting left out, the silent treatment, and a whole list of friendship challenges are just a given if you have girl chemicals popping around in your body. Since those chemicals might have just gotten swirled around by the story about being left out, let's take a brain break and do a Puzzle Craze.

PUZZLE craze

Look at this drawing of four great friends from the True Girl fiction series. Using the descriptions below, try to figure out which girl is which. I did the first one for you.

	Danika is wearing a headband.	Kate is wearing glasses.	Toni is wearing a necklace without a drop.	Yuzi is wearing a crop top.
Yuzi	no			
Toni	no			
Danika	YES!			
Kate	no			

A Girl's Guide to Best Friends and Mean Girls

Even these fictional girls—who love each other like crazy—run into friendship problems. You can't really avoid it, my True Girl.

So, what's a girl to do?

Well, let's look at the Best Friend a girl could ever have: Jesus. He is the ultimate friend, and we can learn a lot about friendship by being his friend and becoming like him. In this meditation session, we're going to try to meditate on the question, "How did Jesus pick friends for keeps?"

Dig in
TO STUDY

DIG IN by Studying John 15:9-17

In John 15, Jesus is talking to his closest friends— the 12 disciples—about how to be a good friend. And he says he has a way to measure true friendship. Using your red marker, underline the verse that tells us how to do that. (Hint: look for the word "measure.")

⋯⋯⋯▶ **9** "I have loved you even as the Father has loved me. Remain in my love. **10** When you obey me, you remain in my love, just as I obey my Father and remain in his love. **11** I have told you this so that you will be filled with my joy. Yes, your joy will overflow!

12 I command you to love each other in the same way that I love you.

13 And here is how to measure it—the greatest love is shown when people lay down their lives for their friends. **14** You are my friends if you obey me. **15** I no longer call you servants, because a master doesn't confide in his servants. Now you are my friends, since I have told you everything the Father told me. **16** You didn't choose me. I chose you.

I appointed you to go and produce fruit that will last, so that the Father will give you whatever you ask for, using my name. **17** I command you to love each other."

Jesus said the measure of true friendship is people "lay[ing] down their lives for their friends." No doubt, he was trying to tell his disciples that he was about to die for them. Why?

The answer is in the most used word in the passage above.

I don't think you'll have any trouble figuring out which word that is. Just look closely. Using your red pen, put a big red heart around it each time it appears.

Fill in the blank.

Jesus laid his life down for his friends because he _____ them.

meditation promise

Remember, God promises us success when we meditate. So, if you meditate on what he says about friendship, you'll see some improvement in your friendships. I promise!

puzzle craze

Five Things Jesus' Disciples Did to Lay Down Their Lives

Okay, so *Jesus* loved his friends enough to die for them. That's something you probably already knew. You didn't have to dig too hard to find that. *But did you know they did the same thing for him?* Jesus' closest friends laid down their lives in many different ways. In this word search, you'll find five things they endured. Find these words:

PRIS?N   LE?T ?A?ILIES   D??T?   L?FT J?B?   B??TI??S

A	B		N	B	R	I	N	O	T	I	G	T	I
P	E	E	E	E	I	E	O	S	B	G	N	P	I	N
R	E	L	A	R		S	I	L	M	I	S	T	A	F
I	E	E	P	T	I	L	E	F	T		J	O	B	S
S	O	F	O	R	I	F		A	L	G		L	I	E
O	N	T	P	E	I	N	E	I	I	A	F	E	R	I
O	E		L	O	P	B	G	S	I	S	A	N	H	E
N	S	J	F		E	I	D	A	E	T	H	T	H	S
T	J	O	A	S	J	D	E	A	T	L	A	F	B	S
	S	M	E	O		N	T	I	S	E	M	I	T	F
L	B	E	A	T	I	N	G	S	D	L	N	A	M	N
A	I	L	E	F	T		F	E	M	I	L	I	E	S
E	L	E	F	T		F	A	M	I	L	I	E	S	G
L	F	R	F	L	E	F	T		J	O	B	J	L	D
S	J	S	O	O	F	M	O	E	A	E	A	F	E

For puzzle answers go to page 111.

Each of the 12 disciples—Jesus' closest friends—left families and jobs. During Christ's life and after it, several of them left friends behind to travel to distant countries. They were often lonely. After Jesus died and came back to life, they were beaten and imprisoned for his sake, and many were killed in terrible ways.

If anyone has ever had friends who were keepers, he did. And I think one way you can have faithful friends is to begin friendships the same way that Jesus did.

Look again at John 15 on pages 53–54. Using your yellow pen, circle the two words in verse 16 that demonstrate how these friendships started.

Now, fill in the blanks.

Jesus' friends didn't _____ him. He _____ them.

Okay, hold that thought, while we look inside you!

LOOK inside yourself

1 Have you ever had any of the following happen to you?

Write yes or no beside each one.

_____ You were the last one picked for a team.

_____ You felt left out because you weren't invited to a sleepover.

_____ No one sat by you at lunch. You sat alone.

_____ No one picked you to hang with after church.

When Jesus said, "I chose you" to his friends, he meant these words for you and me too. Jesus' 12 friends on earth aren't his only friends. So, get this…Jesus picks you. Every time. Every day. He picks you, kid!

2 **How does that make you feel?** Using your colored markers, draw a picture of your emotion in the box below. Select colors that help you express your emotion.

Under the box, name your picture descriptively.

_____

When I think of Jesus picking me as a friend, it makes me feel like I have butterflies in my tummy and confetti popping out of my ears! Whew! Okay, come down from the high. (Boy, this lesson has been a roller-coaster ride for my heart!)

Time out! Our friendship with Jesus is nothing like our friendships with other girls. After all, he is *God*! We're not equal. He deserves and commands our respect, honor, and awe! But it's truly amazing to think that he—our Savior, our Lord, our God—wants us also to have a friendship with him. And I really think there is something for you and me to learn about our friendships with girls when we look at how Jesus started his friendship with the 12 disciples (and you and me). Let's see if we can get there together...

 Circle one of the following to finish the sentence.
When I am just getting started on a friendship I tend to...

A Worry a lot about if the other girl likes me. I wait for her to approach me.

B I don't get too stressed, but I do put out feelers to see if I can gauge how she feels about me. I want her to like me as much as I think I like her. If she acts like she likes me, I might try to get something started.

C I look around to see who needs a friend. Then I choose to pursue her.

Did you select a totally, completely 100 percent honest answer?

········► Okay, now underline the one that looks *most* like Jesus' example.

I really think most girls would have to honestly circle *a* or *b* when they describe how they pick friends. But clearly, Jesus' example is *c*. Most of our friendships don't have much of a chance, because rather than picking friends and focusing on their needs, we're all too focused on worrying if someone is going to pick us! It's all wrong! It's completely backward from Jesus' example. Our friendships are bound to have problems until we fix this.

4 What do you think you need to do based on what you've just studied while "digging in"? (We'll pray about it in just a moment!)

_____

_____

_____

_____

Great work studying today, True Girl. Now it's time to slow down a little and really think about what this all means. Fill in the blanks below prayerfully so that you can pray this prayer out loud and really mean it. You can even add a whole bunch of stuff to these prayers if you feel like it. Just spend a little time talking to God. Without this, you've not truly meditated.

_____

_____

_____

_____

_____

_____

_____

_____

Reach UP TO TalK TO GOD

Dear Jesus, my Best Friend!

I really can't believe you want to be my friend. Thanks for picking me! It makes me feel

_____

when I think about it. I need to ask you to forgive me. I've just realized that when I start a friendship I tend to _____.

I know you want me to be more focused on the needs of others and not my own feelings. Help me to reorganize my mind, and help me to think of someone who needs me to pick her. (Pause and wait for God to talk to you. Just be still and patient!) Wow, God! I thought of

_____.

I really think she needs a friend because _____

_____

_____.

Could you help me to approach her?

In Jesus' name,

_____

(sign here)

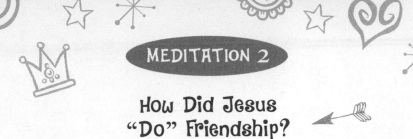

How Did Jesus "Do" Friendship?

you are so not in the mood for excuses and lame apologies. It's the fifth time this afternoon that your little brother has barged in on you and your best friend. This time, he stepped on your school project, and wrinkled the poster board when he jumped through the door wearing nothing but his Elmo boxers, a swim mask, and a Superman cape!

"Ahhhhhhhhhhhh!" you holler. "I...*you*...I can't believe...If you...!"

You search for words to describe your anger, but they don't come out. Suddenly, your BFF swoops in to save the day.

"Little Dude," she says, stepping between the two of you. "What she's trying to say is that she loves you a lot and likes to be near you, but right now we have to get this totally not-fun social-studies poster finished. In fact, we could get it done faster if you would cut out these pictures for us! Take them into your room and use your special scissors."

Little brother pushes his swim mask back on his head, grabs the pictures with wide eyes, and marches off with his important assignment.

"When we're done, we should totally make brownies with him," says your superhero BFF. You know she's just poured cool water on your steaming hot temper and rescued you from saying something you'd regret.

Suddenly you feel so much better!

Maybe your BFF has been taking a look at Jesus' friendships. It sure sounds like it. After Jesus picked his friends for keeps, he knew exactly how to "do" the friendship. He knew what came next. Today we're going to meditate on the question, "How did Jesus 'do' friendship?"

Dig in TO STUDY

DiG In by Studying Luke 10:38-42; John 11:1,3,5-8,14,17,20-23,28-29, 32-36,39-44

Roll up your sleeves. Today you have *a lot* of Bible reading to do. (Remember, this is a *Bible* study, after all!)

Jesus had more than just the 12 disciples for friends. Three of his other friends were especially close. They were Martha, Mary, and Lazarus—two sisters and a brother.

You've probably grown up reading their stories, but today we are going to look past the obvious parts of the story to really be friendship detectives. We're going to look for six things Jesus did in this friendship that you can also do in your friendships. I've underlined the sentences you need to analyze. In the balloon connected to it, I want you to write a contemporary version of what Jesus is doing. I filled in two for you.

Jesus spent a lot of __(**time**)__ with his friends!

Luke 10:38...Jesus and the disciples...

came to a village where a woman named Martha welcomed them

into her home. **39** Her sister, Mary, sat at the Lord's feet, listening to

what he taught.

Jesus __(**told**)__ them what he knew about life and God.

40 But Martha was worrying over the big dinner she was preparing. She came to Jesus and said, "Lord, doesn't it seem unfair to you that my sister just sits here while I do all the work? Tell her to come and help me." **41** <u>But the Lord said to her, "My dear Martha, you are so upset over all these details!</u> **42** There is really only one thing worth being concerned about. Mary has discovered it—and I won't take it away from her."

Jesus _____ his friends get along with each other.

John 11:1 A man named Lazarus was sick. He lived in Bethany with his sisters, Mary and Martha… **3** So the two sisters sent a message to Jesus telling him, "Lord, the one you love is very sick." **5** Although Jesus loved Martha, Mary, and Lazarus, **6** he stayed where he was for the next two days and did not go to them. **7** Finally after two days, he said to his disciples, "Let's go to Judea again." **8** <u>But his disciples objected.</u>

Jesus _____ his own life to help them.

<u>"Teacher," they said, "only a few days ago the Jewish leaders in Judea</u>

were trying to kill you. Are you going there again?"… **14** Then he told

them plainly, "Lazarus is dead…" **17** When Jesus arrived at Bethany, he

was told that Lazarus had already been in his grave for four days…

20 When Martha got word that Jesus was coming, she went to meet

him. But Mary stayed at home. **21** Martha said to Jesus, "Lord, if you had

been here, my brother would not have died. **22** But even now I know

that God will give you whatever you ask." **23** Jesus told her, "Your

brother will rise again"… **28** Then she left him and returned to Mary.

She called Mary aside from the mourners and told her, "The Teacher is

here and wants to see you." **29** So Mary immediately went to him…

32 When Mary arrived and saw Jesus, she fell down at his feet and

said, "Lord, if you had been here, my brother would not have died."

33 When Jesus saw her weeping and saw the other people wailing

with her, he was moved with indignation and was deeply troubled.

34 "Where have you put him?" he asked them. They told him, "Lord,

come and see." **35** <u>Then Jesus wept.</u>

Jesus _____
with and for his friends.

36 The people who were

standing nearby said, "See

how much he loved him"…

39 "Roll the stone aside," Jesus told them.

But Martha, the dead man's sister, said, "Lord, by now the smell will be terrible because he has been dead for four days."

Jesus _____ for his friends.

40 Jesus responded, "Didn't I tell you that you will see God's glory if you believe?" **41** So they rolled the stone aside. Then Jesus looked up to heaven and said, "Father, thank you for hearing me. **42** You always hear me, but I said it out loud for the sake of all these people standing here, so they will believe you sent me." **43** Then Jesus shouted, "Lazarus, come out!" **44** And Lazarus came out.

Jesus slept over at Martha, Mary, and Lazarus' house. He spent a lot of time with them. He taught them how to live and have a relationship with God, his Father. He helped Martha and Mary solve their problem. He went out of his way to help his friend, Lazarus. He cried with and for them. He prayed for Lazarus.

What are the six things you and I can do? The list might look like this. See if you can fill in the blanks.

1. Spend a lot of _____ with friends.

2. _____ them what you know about life and God.

3. Help my friends _____ _____ with each other.

4. Take time to _____ them.

5. _____ with and for them.

6. _____ for them.

Why Did Jesus "Do" Friendship the Way He Did? Unscramble the following words.

Puzzle craze

SJUES VLODE ATHRMA, YMRA, DAN ZARSULA!

_____ _____ _____,

_____, _____ _____.

(John 12:5)

For puzzle answers go to page 111.

That takes us back to our first meditation when we looked at why Jesus picked friends for keeps. He loved them. He picked his friends (including you) because of love. And, he does friendship the way he does out of love!

He is not only our greatest friend, but since he is perfect, he models great friendship for us. Speaking of which, let's take a look inside you!

**LOOK
inside
yourself**

1 Using all your markers, draw a picture of you and your BFF in the box below. If you have a great photo, you can just paste it there.

2 Let's see if you're modeling Jesus' example of friendship with her. **Check the appropriate box.**

	Totally! Got it covered!	Oops! I don't do this!	Hmm? Could do better.
I teach her what I know about life and God.	♥		
I spend a lot of time with her.			♥
I get in the middle of her fights to solve them.	♥		
I take risks to help her.			
I cry with and for her.		♥	
I pray for her.			

3 Based on your responses, write two goals that will help you to be more like Jesus in the way you "do" friendship with your BFF.

Goal #1 _____

_____

_____

_____

Goal #2 _____

_____

_____

_____

Okay, you've studied the Bible, but now it's time to pray and ask God to let what's in your head sink into your heart. Without this important step of pausing to consider what God wants to say to us, we risk becoming proud about how much we know about God without ever feeling the beauty of his friendship.

Reach UP TO TALK TO GOD

Dear Jesus,

What a great friend you are! I never really thought about all of those things you did to be a great friend to Martha, Mary, and Lazarus. Those are good ideas for me in my friendships. I was especially amazed to learn that you _____ _____.

My best friend is _____ but you already know that. Two goals I have are to _____ _____ and to _____ _____. Please make me want to do this.

In Jesus' name,

_____

(sign here)

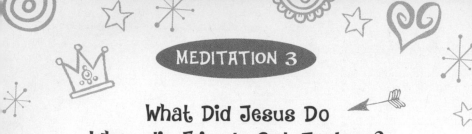

What Did Jesus Do When His Friends Got Jealous?

It's Monday at lunch and things aren't going too well. None of your friends are acting right. It all started when you walked out of homeroom with Miss New Girl. Your BFF looked at you like you had slapped her. You were just trying to be nice! Now, she's sitting with someone else and that someone else's BFF at lunch. You hear them whispering over their PB and Js.

Wait! Did you just hear your name? Maybe they're going to invite you over. Nope! They're laughing now. Is it possible they're laughing *at* you? An internal girls-only alarm system goes off in your heart. It's a BFF takeover—a three-friend gang-up!

Easy now…breathe!

Do your friends ever get jealous? Do you?

Guess what? So did Jesus' friends. James and John were two of Jesus' closest friends. (Only Peter enjoyed as close a friendship.) But once, those two best buddies almost caused a complete friendship meltdown in the inner circle of Jesus' 12 closest friends. Today we're going to meditate on the question, "What did Jesus do when his friends got jealous?"

Dig in TO STUDY

DIG IN by Studying Matthew 20:20-28

It all started when James and John's mama arrived on the scene. She apparently had noticed that Jesus was especially close to her boys. Maybe she also knew that he liked Peter a lot. Perhaps she grew jealous. But the bottom line is she got a crazy idea and headed out to ask Jesus what he thought about it. Underline her idea on the next page using your green-with-envy marker.

········▶ **Matthew 20:20** Then the mother of James and John, the

sons of Zebedee, came to Jesus with her sons. She knelt respectfully

to ask a favor. **21** "What is your request?" he asked. She replied, "In your

Kingdom, will you let my two sons sit in places of honor next to you,

one at your right and the other at your left?"... **23** [Jesus said,] "But I

have no right to say who will sit on the thrones next to mine. My Father

has prepared those places for the ones he has chosen." **24** When the

ten other disciples heard what James and John had asked, they were

indignant. **25** But Jesus called them together and said, "You know

that in this world kings are tyrants, and officials lord it over the people

beneath them. **26** But among you it should be quite different. Whoever

wants to be a leader among you must be your servant, **27** and whoever

wants to be first must become your slave. **28** For even I, the Son

of Man, came here not to be served but to serve others,

and to give my life as a ransom for many."

You should have underlined "In your Kingdom, will you let my two sons sit in places of honor next to you, one at your right and the other at your left?" Basically, Mom decides that James and John deserve to be in the two closest positions of honor to Jesus. But did she come to that all on her own? Nope. She was just the designated spokesperson.

Read verse 20 and use your green-with-envy marker to circle the three words that tell you who came to Jesus with her.

Seems like James and John had a little something to do with this plot to rule the kingdom of God. They'd made a plan that left everyone else out and created a really nasty emotion in the other disciples.

Read verse 24. Put a green-with-envy box around the word that describes how the other ten disciples felt.

puzzle craze

Some Other Words for "Indignant"

Indignant. That's how the other ten disciples felt when they found out James and John had sought out this special honor. *They disrupted the careful balance of friendship in their little group by weighing their own value against the others.* There are six words in the word search below that describe what it means to feel indignant. Start with the first letter. Cross out the letter A and continue to cross out every other letter to find six words that describe "indignant."

AIZNTSGUVLRTQETDXMRASDVICNVFRUWRSI
DARTTEWDMRREKSHEYNUTIFRUWLEJ
FEGAQLJOBUCSEOUFIFEEHNKDZEED

1. ___ ___ ___ ___ ___ ___ ___ ___

  2. ___ ___ ___

3. ___ ___ ___ ___ ___ ___ ___

  4. ___ ___ ___ ___ ___ ___ ___ ___

   5 . ___ ___ ___ ___ ___ ___ ___ ___

  6. ___ ___ ___ ___ ___ ___ ___ ___

For puzzle answers go to page 111.

Bible scholars (older dudes who study the Bible like crazy) say what happened with the disciples was pretty ugly. It included nasty gestures, like giving James and John dirty looks or turning their backs to them. It also included angry words that probably grew to out-of-control yelling. James and John never should have tried to make themselves to be of more value. It only added jealousy to their side of the scale, and things got so out of hand that it looked a lot more like mean-girl chaos than the meeting of God's 12 choice followers.

Speaking of which, let's take a look inside you!

LOOK inside yourself

Even though jealousy is a sin we have all committed, most of us don't like to admit we struggle with it (or create it). We end up "weighing" ourselves against each other when we make comparisons—or competing, like James and John did.

1 First, write your name in the left label of the scale below. Write your BFF's name on the center label. Now, think of the name of someone who is also your BFF's friend but not really yours. Write her name on the right label of the scale.

YOUR NAME

BFF'S FRIEND'S NAME

YOUR BFF'S NAME

2 Read the phrases below and put an "x" beside any of the ones you have thought when you think about your BFF's other friend.

_____ I wonder who my BFF likes better. **(sad)**

_____ But I've known my BFF longer than she has!

_____ I wonder if she is more fun than I am?

_____ I'm just not going to be friends with either of them!

_____ Am I losing my BFF?

Now, using only the statements you've marked, write a word beside it describing how you feel when you think that thought. I did the first one so you have an example. If I thought, *I wonder who my BFF likes better*, it would make me sad.

I wonder who my BFF likes better

Take those words and write them on the scale above your name.

3 What happens to the delicate balance of friendship when you weigh your value against another person's? Circle one:

A Nothing—life is great and we all get to eat Nerds.

B The "other girl" gets weighed down by my ugly feelings.

C My best friend feels stuck in the middle.

D I get weighed down by my ugly feelings.

Not only does your BFF feel torn, but you get to carry the heavy weight of those ugly emotions created by jealousy. Not your friend—not your friend's other friend. *You*. You get to carry the ugly emotions around.

4 **Jesus' approach to jealousy was unlike ours.** He basically said, "Hey, kings were created to fight battles, but you guys were created to be friends. Friends don't do this. They serve each other. Even I came to serve." Seems like the best solution to a jealously triangle is to do something to serve the person you're jealous of. What is something nice that you can do for your BFF's other friend? Using the "How-can-I-serve-you?" Chatterbox on page 76, write some ideas in the triangles for how you can serve your BFF's other friend. I got you started with a few ideas.

After you write on your chatterbox and get it operating, come back to page 79 and finish this fun lesson.

What is something nice you can do for your BFF's other friend?

The "How-can-I-serve-you" Chatterbox

After you write in your ideas for serving, use these directions to fold your Chatterbox and use it.

1. Cut out the big square. Fold and unfold it in half diagonally in both directions to make an X. Place the square picture-side down.

2. Fold each corner to point into the center.

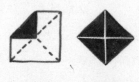

3. Flip so that the flaps are facedown. Then fold each corner to the center.

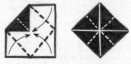

4. Fold in half this way to crease.

5. Then unfold and fold in half the other way.

6. Stick both thumbs and pointer fingers into the four pockets. Push all the pockets to a point to begin playing.

A Girl's Guide to Best Friends and Mean Girls

3

lunch

meditate

Help her with her homework.

Organize her desk during recess.

4

friend

Jesus

Bake her some cookies.

cookie

email

Paint her fingernails.

puzzle

Dig-in

6

7

········► To Play Chatterbox

Take your chatterbox to school or church and ask your BFF to use it to help you pick something neat you can do for her friend…who may soon become yours!

1. Insert your fingers and thumbs under the numbered flaps on the chatterbox.

2. Ask your BFF's friend to choose a number from one of the outside flaps, or choose one yourself. Open and close your fingers that number of times, moving your fingers from front to back and then sideways.

3. Have your friend choose one of the words on the inside of the chatterbox. Spell out the word, opening and closing your fingers with each letter.

4. Ask your friend to pick one of the words that shows. Open that flap and read what you get to do to serve her. And then do it!

It's time to pray! You know how important this is, right? Don't fall for the trap of thinking you've finished just because you've studied hard. Checking in with God seals all that you just stuffed into your brain…and gets it down to your heart!

Reach up to Talk to God

Dear Jesus,

Wow! I can't believe that even your closest friends struggled with jealousy. When I think about this, I have to say

_____

_____

_____

God, I'm really struggling a little bit myself. Here's what you need to know about it. _____

_____

_____

_____

_____

When I wrote the ideas of how I can serve this person, it made me feel _____

_____.

Please open up doors for me to serve her and help my BFF to understand how much I need her help.

In Jesus' name,

_____

(sign here)

MEDITATION 4

What Did Jesus Do When His Friends Hurt Him?

Check out this terrible scene!

You walk into the bathroom at church and you hear two voices chatting. You immediately recognize one of them as the voice of your good friend. You're just about to pipe up and say "hi" when the voice you don't recognize says something that could make the rays of the sun freeze!

"I hear [insert your name here] is totally annoying. Do you know her?" The words echo off the metal bathroom doors and pierce your heart. Silence follows.

"Uh, no," you hear your friend say. "I don't know her...much."

You slink out of the bathroom with tears burning your eyes. What should you do next?

Well, how about we take a look at what Jesus did! If James and John were two of his closest friends, the only other was Peter. Guess what Peter did? He denied he was ever friends with Jesus. Today, we're going to meditate on the question, "What did Jesus do when his friends hurt him?"

Dig in
TO STUDY

DIG IN by Studying John 18:15-17,25-27

Peter denied he was Jesus' friend. Look at the passage on the next page to find out how many times Peter did this. Use your I'm-so-blue marker to circle each incident.

John 18:15 Simon Peter followed along behind, as did another of the disciples. That other disciple was acquainted with the high priest, so he was allowed to enter the courtyard with Jesus.

16 Peter stood outside the gate. Then the other disciple spoke to the woman watching at the gate, and she let Peter in. **17** The woman asked Peter, "Aren't you one of Jesus' disciples?" "No," he said, "I am not"...

25 Meanwhile, as Simon Peter was standing by the fire, they asked him again, "Aren't you one of his disciples?" "I am not," he said.

26 But one of the household servants of the high priest, a relative of the man whose ear Peter had cut off, asked, "Didn't I see you out there in the olive grove with Jesus?" **27** Again Peter denied it. And immediately a rooster crowed.

How many times did Peter say he wasn't Jesus' friend? Write the answer on the line below.

 _____

what did Jesus do?

Dude! That must have hurt bad. I don't know about you, but I'd have had a massive cry fest! This was one of Jesus' three closest friends, and he said he wasn't Jesus' friend *three* times! What did Jesus do? Let's check it out. But first, a quick timeline.

puzzle craze

Create a Timeline of Jesus and Peter's Friendship Crisis

Using the line below, add in the proper order these important events that happened between the time that Peter denied Jesus and the time that Jesus caught up with him for their first interaction. Draw pictures to symbolize these three events, taking care to unscramble the order!

♥ Jesus Is Buried in a Tomb
♥ Jesus Dies on the Cross
♥ Jesus Rises from the Dead

1	2	3	4	5

Peter Denies Jesus

Jesus Meets Peter

draw

pictures

here

For puzzle answers go to page 111.

Now, read the exciting first interaction between Jesus and Peter. It's the first time they've had one-on-one interaction since Peter has said three times he was not Jesus' friend. I find four things Jesus does for Peter. See if you can find them. Let's put away that "I'm-so-blue" marker and trade it for a happy sunshine yellow. Circle four things Jesus does for Peter.

·········► John 21:1-13,15,19

1 Later Jesus appeared again to the disciples beside the Sea of Galilee. This is how it happened. **2** Several of the disciples were there—[including] Peter… **3** Simon Peter said, "I'm going fishing." "We'll come, too," they all said. So they went out in the boat, but they caught nothing all night. **4** At dawn the disciples saw Jesus standing on the beach, but they couldn't see who he was. **5** He called out, "Friends, have you caught any fish?" "No," they replied. **6** Then he said, "Throw out your net on the right-hand side of the boat, and you'll get plenty of fish!" So they did, and they couldn't draw in the net because there were so many fish in it. **7** Then the disciple whom Jesus loved said to Peter, "It is the Lord!" When Peter heard that it was the Lord, he…jumped into the water, and swam ashore… **9** When [he] got there, [he] saw that a charcoal fire was burning and fish were frying over it, and there was bread. **10** "Bring some of the fish you've just caught," Jesus said.

11 So Simon Peter went aboard and dragged the net to the shore. There were 153 large fish, and yet the net hadn't torn. **12** "Now come and have some breakfast!" Jesus said… **13** Then Jesus served them the bread and the fish… **15** After breakfast Jesus said to Simon Peter, "Simon son of John, do you love me more than these?" "Yes, Lord," Peter replied, "you know I love you"… **19** …Then Jesus told him, "Follow me."

Jesus helped Peter and the others catch an enormous load of fish. He built Peter a nice, cozy campfire to cuddle up next to. He served him breakfast. And he invited him to follow him—to once again be his friend. In fact, Jesus made Peter a leader of the church and called him "the Rock"!

Is that what you would have done? Let's look inside.

LOOK inside yourself

1 **Have any of these things ever happened to you?** Put an "x" beside any that have.

_____ You invite a friend over and she says she has to stay home, but then you find out she accepted an invitation to another girl's house.

_____ You tell your friend a secret, and then you find out she told everyone else.

_____ You catch two of your friends laughing at you when something bad happens.

_____ Miss Born-to-Be-Mean blames you *in front of everyone* for losing the soccer game. Your BFF doesn't defend you.

_____ You buy a shirt you really like. You told your friend you were going to buy it. She goes out and buys the same one even though she knows you don't like it when she does that.

_____ (Add your own here.) _____

_____

_____

_____

 What did you do? Circle all that apply. **Cried.**

TOLD OTHER FRIENDS NOT TO TRUST THAT GIRL.

PROMISED I'D NEVER BE FRIENDS WITH HER AGAIN.

Gave her time to say she was sorry, and she did.

Wrote her a long email asking if everything was cool.

baked her our fav snack and took it to her.

STOMPED OFF AND FOUND A NEW FRIEND TO REPLACE HER.

MADE HER A COZY CAMPFIRE.

Wrote her a long email telling her to forget it!

Look at what you just circled above. Are these things Jesus would have done?

A Girl's Guide to Best Friends and Mean Girls

3 Write a list of four things you can do the next time your friend hurts you, based on Jesus' example.

Jesus' List of To-Do's
for a Friend Who Hurt Him

My List of To-Do's
for a Friend Who Hurts Me

1. Create miraculous catch of fish!

1. _____
   _____

2. Start a roaring campfire!

2. _____
   _____

3. Serve a yummy breakfast!

3. _____
   _____

4. Ask friend to be friends again!

4. _____
   _____

Okay, you know the drill.
It's time to pray!

REACH
UP TO
TALK TO
GOD

♡ ♡ ♡ **Dear Best Friend Jesus,**

It must have really hurt when Peter said he wasn't your friend. I imagine when you found out you probably _____
_____. I've been hurt by friends too. Only I didn't react the same way you did. Instead, I _____
and I _____.

From now on, I intend to respond like you did. Help me to do this. I know it won't be easy.

In Jesus' name,

_____

(sign here)

MEDITATION 5

How Can I Be a Good Friend to Jesus?

School was tough today. One uber-math test plus one essay equals a need for a break this afternoon. You hit the kitchen first for a tall glass of milk and some cookies, and then you escape to your bedroom for some serious refueling. But Mom has different plans.

"(Insert your name here), could you come wash the dishes for me? I'm running behind," she calls just as you're about to flop onto your bed with a good book. Something inside of you boils, and you want to grumble. Then you think better and decide you won't grumble, you'll just *explain* why you can't do it. But you quickly come to your senses and drag yourself downstairs, where you are greeted by a tower of soap bubbles that you're certain could top Mt. Everest. You just hope the dishes aren't stacked that high.

enjoying a friendship with my mom

You dive into the task while your mom is folding laundry behind you. Making an intentional effort to be obedient seems to have opened the door of your heart…and your mom's! Before you know it, you and your mom are laughing and talking together. You are enjoying *friendship* with your mom.

I hope this story helps you take a look at an even more unique friendship—friendship with Jesus! Today we're going to meditate on the question, "How can I be a good friend to Jesus?"

DIG IN by Studying John 15:9-17

This is going to sound really familiar. It's the passage we started with. (Remember, it brought us the exciting news that Jesus "picked" us to be friends!) It's a great place to go back to in our study on friendship. Why? Because Jesus clearly tells us how we can be his friend. Using a rainbow of colors, draw a rainbow over the four words that tell us what we must do to be Jesus' friend. (Hint: It begins, "You are my friends...")

Dig in
TO STUDY

········► **John 15:9** "I have loved you even as the Father has loved me. Remain in my love. **10** When you obey me, you remain in my love, just as I obey my Father and remain in his love. **11** I have told you this so that you will be filled with my joy. Yes, your joy will overflow! **12** I command you to love each other in the same way that I love you. **13** And here is how to measure it—the greatest love is shown when people lay down their lives for their friends. **14** You are my friends if you obey me.

15 I no longer call you servants, because a master doesn't confide in his servants. Now you are my friends, since I have told you everything the Father told me. **16** You didn't choose me. I chose you. I appointed you to go and produce fruit that will last, so that the Father will give you whatever you ask for, using my name. **17** I command you to love each other."

What does Jesus want us to do? Write it on the line below.

_____

He said one of the ways we show that we are his friends is by obeying him. That's kind of like what happens when you obey your mom. In obeying her, you produce something. What?

Read verse 16 above and circle the word that tells us what our obedience produces. Fill in the blanks.

Obeying Jesus produces_____that will

_____.

The fruit of obedience Jesus was talking about wasn't Chinese lychee, was it? It was fruit like love, joy, peace, patience, kindness, gentleness, goodness, faithfulness, and self-control.

What fruit from the list above do you think you would produce if you did the dishes for your mom when she asked, even though you were totally worn out? Write your idea below:

_____

Maybe you wrote "self-control." That would be a good choice. (But any of them might be logical, so no answer is wrong.) I would say self-control, because you didn't express your frustration and exhaustion. You sure could have freaked on her, but you didn't. You were self-controlled. You obeyed, and that produced *self-control*, which produced *peace*, which made your *joy* even greater. And that sets the stage for you to interact not only as mother and daughter, but as friends.

How is this a lot like what happens when we obey Jesus? To find out, let's take a look inside of you!

LOOK
inSide
yourself
♡ ♡ ♡

1 Think of something Jesus told you to do, *but you did not obey.* (Some ideas might include inviting the new girl to sit with you, taking out the trash when your mom told you to, or telling a friend you were sorry for something you did.) In the boxes below, draw a four-scene cartoon dramatization.

2 What "fruit" came out of that experience? Circle all that apply.

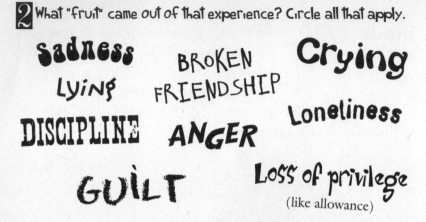

sadness **BROKEN** **Crying**
Lying **FRIENDSHIP**
DISCIPLINE **ANGER** **Loneliness**
GUILT **Loss of privilege**
(like allowance)

Just like our moms or dads have to move into the role of discipliner (taking away privileges like allowance or free time) or teacher (showing us how to respond differently) when we disobey them, Jesus has to do the same. Why? He loves us! They also might have to be our comforter (when we cry). The role they are forced to operate in when you disobey is not that of friend, is it? Circle one.

┄┄┄► YES   NO ◄┄┄┄

3 Now, think of a time when you clearly obeyed Jesus. (Ideas might include turning off the TV to go help your mom set the table, giving up an afternoon to visit your sick grandma, or getting up early to read your Bible.) Using the cartoon strip below, draw a picture of that story.

4 Using your list of fruit from the crossword puzzle on the next page, which ones did you experience as a result of obeying? Write them below.

♥ _____

♥ _____

♥ _____

♥ _____

Obedience created that fruit in your life! It also opened the door for you to be Jesus' friend. It's not that Jesus doesn't want to be your friend when you disobey. But, just like with your mom and dad, your obedience opens the door for laughter, fellowship, and friendship. Can you understand how that works now? Good! Let's pray about it.

What kind of fruit was Jesus talking about?

Puzzle craze

Was Jesus talking about the brown, wrinkly fruit that grows in the Middle East (where he lived) called a date? Ew! Yuck. Of course not! Complete the crossword puzzle by selecting the kind of fruit that you think Jesus was talking about in John 15.

Each word is one of the

_____ of the Spirit.

⟶ CLUES

ACROSS

3. A bouncy bundle of joy or a little orange kumquat.
4. Some kindness or a tart little star fruit.
5. Peace that passes understanding or a kiwi.
6. Some serious self-control or a guava from Mexico.

DOWN

1. A dose of goodness or a bowl of Chinese lychee.
2. Gentleness or a sweet honeydew melon.
7. A bunch of love or a big juicy watermelon.

For puzzle answers go to page 111.

Good work, my STUDIER! Now, let's be a PRAY-ER! Remember, it's when the two of them crash into each other that you're a MEDITATOR!

Reach UP TO TALK TO GOD

Dear Jesus,

I really do want to be your friend. I:

_____ never knew I needed to obey you to be your friend.

_____ already knew I needed to obey you to be your friend.

In thinking about it today, I know:

_____ I need to work on this. I'm not very obedient.

_____ I need to be more consistent. I obey sometimes, but not always.

_____ I'm trying. I think I'm usually obedient.

Of course, everybody needs a little help in some area. I need help _____

_____.

As a matter of a fact, right now when I pray about being obedient, I find myself thinking that I need to _____

_____.

I'm going to get started on that right away.

In Jesus' name,

_____

(sign here)

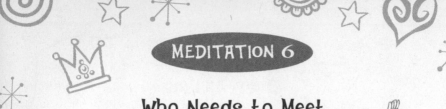
Who Needs to Meet My Friend Jesus?

I t's only the first week of summer and you've already turned your hair green from the chlorine in the pool, pulled enough weeds from your mom's flower bed to fill a small state, and given your dog six bubble baths. Now, you're bored.

But today, you made a fabulous new friend at church. And just in time.

The new girl? She's practically your emotional twin. She loves dogs. So do you. She loves chocolate chip ice cream. So do you. She's totally into Nick at Nite. So are you. She's in dance. So are you. It's like she was made to be your friend.

You race up to your mom with her. Jumping up and down like you're on an invisible pogo stick, you ask, "Mom! Can we have a sleepover? Pleeeease!"

When we find a new friend, we just can't wait to show the person off. We act a little insane sometimes. Are you ever a little insane about sharing your friendship with Jesus? In this meditation we'll explore the question, "Who needs to meet my friend Jesus?"

Dig in
TO STUDY

DIG IN by Studying Luke 12:4-8; Hebrews 7:25; John 17:20; Romans 8:34

Before we look at who needs to meet your friend Jesus, let's take a minute to remember who picked whom to be friends. Fill in the blanks.

I didn't _____ Jesus. He _____ me!

Jesus picked you! Why? *Because he loves you.*

I remember the day that Jesus "picked" me. I was only four and a half. (If I really think hard about it and look in my Bible, I realize that Jesus "picked me" before the world was created! Whoa!) But it was on that day that I decided to respond and to ask him to live in my heart. Have you done that? Oh, I hope so! If you have, write the story of that day in the space below:

If you haven't, turn to page 109 to hear my whole story! After you read it come back to this page! I'll be waiting!

Okay, did you write your story or read mine? If you read mine, maybe you prayed to ask Jesus to be the God of your life! Guess what? You get to go back and write about it above.

I hope you've made that decision to follow Jesus. I hope you love him, because he sure does love you! Just how much? Check it out. Circle the greeting Jesus uses below.

·········► Luke 12:4-8

"Dear friends… **6** What is the price of five sparrows?

A couple of pennies? Yet God does not forget a single one of them.

7 And the very hairs on your head are all numbered.

So don't be afraid; you are more valuable to him than a

whole flock of sparrows. **8** And I assure you of this:

If anyone acknowledges me publicly here on earth,

I, the Son of Man, will openly acknowledge that person

in the presence of God's angels."

Right off the bat, he calls us friends! Cool, huh?

Now, find the two things in verses 6–7 that Jesus says he values to the point of never forgetting. Using any markers you want, draw a picture of each of them directly above the word.

Jesus says he will never forget even the tiniest of sparrows. And then he says that he even has something on you numbered. What? Write it below.

 _____

Why don't you just grab a little bunch of your hair and try to count it? Go ahead. Circle your estimate of how many hairs you have below.

816 **67** **100,000**

200,002 **58,132** **32**

175,739 **99** **87½**

Did you guess 100,000? You're probably close. It varies based on a lot of factors, including hair color.

Based on hair color and estimates, the True Girl fiction characters have this many hairs on their heads:

People with black hair have about 108,000.

People with brown hair have about 100,000.

People with blonde hair have about 140,000.

I guess the point to that verse is that it would be really insanely crazy to keep track of how many hairs are on everyone's head. So, God must be crazy in love with us, huh?

Now, look at verse 8 and circle the thing that Jesus does for us because of his crazy love for us! Fill in the blank below:

"If anyone _____ me publicly here on earth,

I, the Son of Man, will openly _____

that person in the presence of God's angels."

Jesus said that he "acknowledges us" in the presence of God's angels. The word "acknowledge" means "to speak out freely"!

He talks about you! He wants to. It freely flows out of his mouth. (Kind of like when you find a new friend and can't wait to tell her about Jesus.) He is totally telling all the angels and God the Father about you.

Wait. Jesus is talking about you? Really?

Yes, really! Even when Jesus was on this earth praying for his 12 closest friends, he was also praying for Y-O-U! He said so himself. Check it out. Circle the word that represents both you and me if you have asked Jesus to live in your heart.

········▶ **John 17:20**

"I am praying not only for these disciples

but also for all who will ever believe in me

because of their testimony."

Did his prayers end when he ascended into heaven? No way! Circle the word at the top of the next page that tells you how long he'll be praying for you.

········► Hebrews 7:25

"He is able, once and forever, to save everyone

who comes to God through him. He lives forever

to plead with God on their behalf."

He will be praying for you forever! That's a long, long time. And make no mistake who he's talking to. Circle who all this "free speaking" about you is directed to.

········► Romans 8:34

"He is the one who died for us and was

raised to life for us and is sitting at the place of

highest honor next to God, pleading for us."

It feels wonderful to know that Jesus is talkin' about you and me to God the Father! Guess what? Jesus likes it when we approach our friendship with him the same way. Go back to our main passage from Luke on page 98 and find the word that is highlighted. Write it in big letters below.

_If_ we speak out freely for him, then he will speak out freely for us! The gift of God's love and salvation is free. To live in his constant protection and provision depends at least in part on how much we live for him. Are you talking _about_ him? Are you freely speaking about him in front of friends, family, and classmates?

Our A-MAZE-ing Jesus!

Here are some fun and easy ways to "speak out freely" for Jesus! Help True Girl Toni find her way to God's throne by choosing to do simple things that speak out for Jesus.

PuZZLe craze

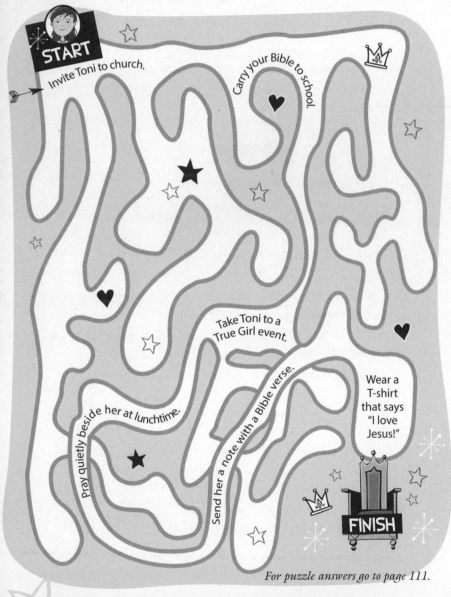

START

Invite Toni to church.

Carry your Bible to school.

Take Toni to a True Girl event.

Pray quietly beside her at lunchtime.

Send her a note with a Bible verse.

Wear a T-shirt that says "I love Jesus!"

FINISH

For puzzle answers go to page 111.

A Girl's Guide to Best Friends and Mean Girls

LOOK inside yourself

1 **Your story of meeting Jesus and deciding to make him the God of your life is the most important story you'll ever tell.** And you should speak freely about it. (I hope you've met Jesus. I hope you do know that you are his and he is your God! If you're not sure, check out page 109!) Use the space below to write out how you decided to become a Christian.

_____

_____

_____

_____

_____

I wish I could read that. I bet it's a great story!

2 **At the top of each of the columns in this chart, write the name of at least one friend who you know has never really met Jesus.** This person isn't "friends" with him. (If you think all of your friends know Jesus, go ahead and write the names of some of them. We should be helping them grow closer to our Best Friend, Jesus!)

1._____ 2._____ 3._____

3 What have you done to tell them about Jesus?

_____

_____

_____

_____

_____

4 What do you think God wants you to do to tell them about Jesus? Using the box with your friends' names, go ahead and write in some ideas.

Reach
UP TO
TalK TO
GOD

Okay. Are you ready for this?
I'm going to let you write your whole letter to God today. No help at all. Just look in your heart and ask him how you can pray into your life the Scripture verses you just studied. Ready? Go! It's time to pray!

Dear _____

_____

_____

_____

_____

puzzle craze

Crazy-for-Jesus Coupons

It's actually easy to share your love for Jesus. You just show kindness and do it in his name. Here's an easy way to do it. Pick two people to bless with these cool coupons. Just ask God to help you decide who you can give them to, and present them as soon as possible.

Get Well Soon!

MISSED YOU at school today, and here are some **HIGHS** and **LOWS** that you missed. *I'm praying for you.*

♥ Assignments: . . . .

. . . .

. . . .

♥ News (Highs & Lows): . . . .

. . . .

. . . .

. . . .

"And [Jesus] healed people who had every kind of sickness and disease"
(Matthew 4:23)

Sweet Surprise!

Here's a candy bar that's as sweet as **YOU** are.

Have a great day, friend!

"The heartfelt counsel of a friend is as sweet as perfume and incense" (Proverbs 27:9).

TO: ....

FROM: ....

Get Well Soon!

To: ....

From: ....

sweet!

Do You Know Jesus?

I remember the day that I began my friendship with Jesus. I was four and a half years old. I was at a neighborhood Bible club, where I had just heard that Jesus loved me and had died for me on the cross.

⤍ John 3:16 says,

"God so loved the world that he gave his only Son, so that everyone who believes in him will not perish but have eternal life."

The teacher told me that the reason Jesus had to die is because God is pure and holy and perfect and can't be near anything that is not. So, he can't be near sin. (Sinning is doing something bad or against God's plan.)

⤍ Romans 3:23

"All have sinned and fall short of God's glorious standard."

Any sin—even just one little one—separates us from God's perfection. I didn't want that. But I knew I had sinned. I wanted to live forever in heaven with Jesus, so I prayed a prayer that sounded a little like this:

"Dear Jesus—
I know I have sinned. I know that this means I cannot live with you in heaven forever. I also know that you died to take the punishment for my sins. Will you forgive me? Come into my heart and be the God of my life. From this day forward, I want to be your friend.
In Your name,
Amen!"

I still remember what things were like that day. I remember the crack in the sidewalk that I saw as I prayed with my eyes open. I remember the smell of the evergreen trees nearby. I treasure that memory, and I know it was the beginning of my friendship with Jesus.

If you have never prayed a prayer like that, you can do it right now. Go get your mom or a teacher if you want someone to pray with you. But don't delay. Jesus wants to be your Best Friend!

Extra Ideas for Bible Study

You can do part 2, the True Girl Bible study, all alone if you want to. But we have some other ideas for you in case you'd like to be creative:

True Girl Online Bible Study: We at True Girl, love studying the Bible so much that we offer online Bible studies for you and your mom. Our biggest one yet had about 5,000 girls and moms joining us from all over the world! Go to mytruegirl.com to learn more.

Mother-Daughter Bible Study: Your mom will learn as much as you will. You see, it's not me teaching—it's God. His Spirit is fully capable of helping your mom to meditate in a way that teaches her as she leads you. To do this with your mom, just get two copies and dig in. You can do it once a week or you can do it every day for a week.

Small Group or Sunday School: How fun would it be to discuss all the great things you learn each week? You can do that by grabbing a group of friends to do this with. Do it after school once a week or in Sunday school every Sunday. We like to keep things simple with True Girl Bible studies, so you really don't need any extra books. If you're the leader, just select one appropriate question from each of the three sections:

- ♥ Dig In to Study
- ♥ Look Inside Yourself
- ♥ Reach Up to Pray

Be sure to enjoy some fun snacks at the beginning and to end in prayer!